To Max & Ginger Johnson
w/ compliments
Gordon Bell
7 - 26 - 10

A COWBOY GOES TO INDIA

THE JOURNAL OF GORDON & LOLA BELL

To: NWHF   5-12-12

GORDON W BELL

xulon
PRESS

TABLE OF CONTENTS

Title Page i
Copyright Page.. ii
Introduction... ix
List of photographs x
Dedication xi
Acknowledgements.. xiii

Lola's Story..17
    Gordon's Story..24
    The Big Move...32
    The Strawstack Adventure............................37
    Jimmy 40
    The Drought Years.....................................48
    Powder River Bob 56
    Taylor University.......................................63
    Extracurricular Activities.............................68
    Pastoral Ministry at Taylor 73
    Fountain City, Gordon's Babyhood 74
    Lola's Memories of Larry's Babyhood..........77
    Wilmore Kentucky.....................................80
    Lola's Memories of Wesley's Babyhood........81
    Life in Lansford, North Dakota 82
    Lola's Memories of Verle's Babyhood 86
    The Transition to India 92

Candidate School 93
Life in Detroit, Michigan 93
Ministry at Stone Chapel 94
Hope Renewed...95
Getting Ready to Go 96
The Fire...98
The First Trip 102
Lola's View of Travel on a P & O Boat 107
Stops Along The Way 108
First Impressions of India 112
Boarding School 121
Language School 123
Our First Hill Season 126
More Language Study 130
Our First Station — Adilabad..................................136
Hot Season and Hill Season — 1954.......................143
Our Chosen Strategy for Village Evangelism............150
Christmas Celebration at Adilabad..........................152
The Model A Ford...158
More Highlights From Our First Term 162
Our First Furlough 170
At The Crossroads 179
Final Years In The India Mission.............................181
The Move To Clancullen 186
Lola's Memories of Clancullen 191
Gordon's Role as Housefather................................193
An Event That Changed Our Lives 196
Early Years At Wun 199
Our First Christmas in Maharashtra 200
Touring In The Villages 202
Hot Season Break In Kodaikanal.............................208
Annual trek to Elephant Valley................................209
October Tours 210
The Boys Come Home For Christmas.......................211
The Mud House In Sunna.......................................213

The Year 1962...215
The Visit To Agra And The Taj Mahal.......................218
Some Time In Seattle......................................223
The Break Up Of The Family................................224
1965 Hill Season..226
Transition From Evangelism to Administration 228
The Move To Umri Hospital.................................229
Vacation Time For Wesley And Verle........................233
Vijay Sidam's Story.......................................233
Bell Family News — 1965...................................235
Teaching At Union Biblical Seminary.......................237
Wesley Graduates from High School 239
June to November 1967.....................................243
Final Months of First Period with The Free
    Methodist Mission 245
Verle Graduates and Leaves With Lola
    For The U.S..248
Five Years in America.....................................252
Some Pastoral Testing Times...............................255
Call To Return To India 257
A Year At Fuller..261
Back To India In 1975 263
The Latter Years of Mission Service 264
Bridges to God..266
The Grand Ceremony Begins 273
Other Missionary Duties...................................278
The Bombay Story..279
Our Work At Union Biblical Seminary 286
The Seminary Moves to Pune................................288
Yavatmal College of Leadership Training...................291
A Snapshot of The Year 1983 299

EPILOGUE..303
   Year of Deputation...303
   Securing Visas for David and Sherrill Yardy..............303
   Adapting to Life in America..................................304
   Fifteen Months in Alaska.....................................304
   Life in Seattle..305
   The Move to Warm Beach.....................................307
   Chaplain of Warm Beach Senior Community...........307
   Family Get-Togethers...307
   Golden Wedding Anniversary................................308
   The Bell Family in 2004.......................................309
   Gordon and Mary's Family....................................309
   Larry and Kimi's Family.......................................309
   Wesley and Jean's Family......................................311
   Verle and Lois's Family..312
   Summary..313

DEVELOPMENTS IN THE FREE METHODIST
CHURCH OF INDIA UP TO 1995 313

   Church Growth...313
   Yavatmal College of Leadership Training................315
   Umri Christian Hospital.......................................315

FURTHER DEVELOPMENTS UP TO 2010.................317

INTRODUCTION

This journal is not organized by chapters. The story will flow from episode to episode and from segment to segment. Each segment has a title. Some readers may wish to read the entire story from beginning to end. Others may prefer to select episodes or segments that interest them. You will find the table of contents helpful for selecting a section of interest or to find the page number of a topic that you wish to go back and review.

Some of the episodes are written from memory. Much of the story is compiled from information contained in our newsletter called "Chimes of India." It was our privilege to serve the Lord over 55 years. Thirty of those years were given to India. The early years of our mission service were with International Missions. More than twenty years were with The Department of World Mission of The Free Methodist

Church. May this account of our life's journey be a blessing, encouragement and inspiration to all who choose to read it.

Still on that journey to heaven that has taken me around the world.

Gordon Bell

LIST OF PICTURES

1. Lola at age five
2. Lola at Taylor
3. Gordon at Taylor
4. Our four sons
5. Map of India
6. Our family at Adilabad
7. Lola with Library staff
8. Gordon with student
9. Golden wedding photograph

DEDICATION

We dedicate this journal to our Lord and Savior Jesus Christ. Our years of service in India were in response to His call.

Secondly, we dedicate this journal to you, our four sons. You made significant sacrifices because of our missionary career. In ways you know and in ways you may not know, you made a contribution to the cause of missions. Without question, you have added much to our lives. We are deeply grateful.

May our story in some way enrich your lives and the lives of future generations of our family.

Lovingly,

Mom and Dad

Grandma and Grandpa

Great Grandma and Great Grandpa

ACKNOWLEDGMENTS

In writing, revising and publishing these memoirs, I received help from a number of people whom I want to acknowledge.

My heartfelt thanks go to my wife Lola, now in heaven, for encouraging me to write this journal. She made valuable suggestions and patiently endured the many hours the project required.

Pauline Todd graciously read the manuscript a few pages at a time as I was writing the rough draft. My apologies to her for not having her do a final reading of the manuscript for the first edition. We rushed to have it ready in time for Lola's and my sixtieth wedding anniversary.

A very big "thank you" goes to Helen Kline who graciously read the manuscript and checked grammar and spelling. Her suggestions for format and structure were priceless. What a giant contribution she has made to the project! Our granddaughter Stephanie Bell read the manuscript and made her valuable suggestions. The final reading was done by Jean Bell, my daughter-in-law, who added her suggestions, which raised questions concerning passages that did not clearly express my thoughts. Her valuable suggestions regarding sentence structure led to a goodly number of improvements.

I have been blessed to have friends and family give such valuable assistance. My loving thanks to each and all.

LOLA AGE 5

LOLA'S STORY

"**D**addy, where did I come from?" Lola used to ask. "Oh, we picked you up on a street corner in Hamtramick," was his humorous reply. Lola Marjorie Kelley was born in Highland Park, Michigan, on August 6, 1920. (Highland Park is a suburb north of Detroit with Woodward Avenue running through its center.) She was the youngest of three living children. Her sister Doris was four and her brother Elvan was twelve when she was born.

Shortly after her birth, the family moved to Detroit's west side. At first they lived in an apartment house. While living in the apartment house, J.L. Kelley built two houses, one for his own family and the other for his sister and brother-in-law Lois and Wilfred Kroh and their family. The house he built for his family was on Lauder Street where Lola and her family lived from 1920 to 1928. (Lauder was located near Strathmoor and Grand River Avenue.)

Mr. Kelley was one of the first contractors in the Detroit area to use a production line method of construction. He would arrange to build all of the houses in a city block simultaneously. In this way he could contract with a crew to dig a number of basements one after another. In a similar fashion the cement workers could use the forms to pour concrete one basement after another. Likewise crews especially trained for the work could most efficiently do each stage that followed. J.L. did very well in this enterprise for some time. However, when the depression came, he was forced into bankruptcy.

Mr. Kelley was not one to give up. As an entrepreneur, he tried several types of businesses including a gas station, and a grocery store, followed by the "Baby Beef Restaurant" in Ferndale. One of the finer houses J. L. had constructed was in Ferndale. The family moved into that lovely home at this time. Lola remembers with delight the time she enjoyed in this elegant, three-bedroom home.

In her lifetime Lola lived in as many as forty-five different places. Her brother Elvan helped her compile a list of the places the family lived during this period of her childhood. First, while operating the duck farm, they lived for a short while on Evergreen Avenue. That year, 1929, they moved to Romulus. In 1930, they moved to Ferndale and

Nine Mile Road. In 1931, they operated an apartment house on Concord, near Belle Isle. However, they moved back to Ferndale in 1932 and lived in a small apartment house.

Mr. Kelley had grown up in the country and was proud that his life was free from tobacco, alcohol and such vices. Just at this time, his friends persuaded him that he could not succeed in the restaurant business unless he served beer. Having failed one time after another before this, he was so desperate to succeed that he agreed to serve alcoholic beverages. His restaurants were successful for a while.

In June 1934, J. L. Kelley suffered a debilitating stroke that brought his business career to an end and soon plunged his family into great difficulty. With J. L. bedridden for nearly a year, the family income was gone and they had no place to live. In the emergency, Lola along with her mother and father moved in with her brother Elvan and his wife Betty, who lived in a large rooming house on Vernor Avenue. Shortly after, her Aunt Lois and Uncle Wilfred Kroh took in her parents. (Lois was J. L.'s sister.) Wilfred and Lois lived in Ferndale and had taken over one of J. L.'s restaurants.

Sometime later Lola went to live with Doris and Woody Hults, her sister and brother-in-law. During this period they found work for Lola with a Catholic family that provided her board and room. Then when things had settled down a little, they remembered that Spotts Farm (Mrs. Kelley's parents' farm) was vacant — her grandparents having passed away several years before this. They took refuge at the farm for the latter part of the summer of 1934. By God's grace the farm was adjacent to the farm of her Uncle Harley and Aunt Cynthia Spotts. (Harley was her mother's brother.) They were a gracious and compassionate Christian couple whose loving care meant a lot at such a difficult time.

Lola remembers attending school on Pleasant Lake Road in the fall of 1934. Her grandparents' farm was on Spotts Road. The school was on the corner of Pleasant Lake and Spotts Roads. One can still find the actual farm and school located in the country about ten miles southeast of Hillsdale, Michigan. Because her parents had probably moved back to Detroit at this time, Lola lived with her Uncle and Aunt for a while.

In 1935, when Lola's father had improved in health, one of the houses he had built. (at 15158 DaCosta in west Detroit) became available after the occupants vacated. So the family was able to locate there, and once they were settled, Lola was able to continue her education at Redford High School.

The houses that became available to the family at this time were blessings that had to be claimed with difficulty. The house on Spotts farm had been standing empty for years. It must have been a colossal task for Mrs. Kelley to make it livable while taking care of an invalid husband. The house on DaCosta was dirty and infested with bed bugs when they took it over. Mrs. Kelley used kerosene around the baseboards and everywhere the vermin could lodge. It took months to eradicate them.

In a year or two the Spotts Farm finally sold. Mrs. Kelley received a share of that estate. Mr. Kelley had recovered sufficiently that he could use those funds and supervise major remodeling of the DaCosta house. The remodeling included construction of a sub-basement with windows above ground. This made it suitable for use as an apartment. Renovations were made so that the family could live downstairs and rent the upstairs for income.

These were difficult years financially. For J. L. Kelley it was torture to have his family on welfare. Lola remembers the embarrassment of having the word "welfare" stamped inside her textbooks. Having to buy shoes with welfare stamps meant buying shoes without any style. Her Mom made her dresses from old material and hand-me-downs. In time her parents were able to manage on their own without welfare. Mrs. Kelley operated a bakery in the front portion of the basement apartment, and Mr. Kelley bought an egg route that he managed with Lola's help. In this way with the rental income they were able to carry on until J.L.'s death in 1939. He was just fifty-four years old when he passed away.

When Lola was about to graduate from the eighth grade, her Dad suffered his first major stroke. The family disruption kept her out of school for a year so that she completed high school five years later. It was just after her graduation from high school that her father passed away. During all of her high school years there had been the distress of moving from one school to another. All of these factors made it difficult for her to get as much out of her education as she might have. However, having to relate to new people and to new situations did help her develop skills that have been useful throughout her life.

Each summer her family went to Hillsdale, Michigan, to visit relatives of both her mother and father. Some of these relatives were committed Christians. In those days her family thought that these relatives were too religious. Be that as it may, through them she began to realize that her loved ones had a wonderful relationship with Christ, and she began to desire this relationship for herself.

At the age of eleven, she visited her Uncle Harley and Aunt Cynthia Spotts, of Osseo, Michigan (Osseo is approximately ten miles east of Hillsdale, Michigan.) During that visit, she went with them to a camp meeting. One night the evangelist invited folks to come forward to accept Jesus as their Savior. Lola remembers going forward at that time, but still did not know what it was all about. It seemed to her like becoming a citizen. From this time onward she began praying — something that was not done in her home. Up to this time, she had not even learned the Lord's Prayer.

Two or three years later her father sought healing from his stroke. Though the Lord did not choose to heal him physically, he found the Lord as his Savior. His testimony was, "The Lord had to lay me on my back to get me to look up." His left side remained paralyzed until his death. Lola was always very close to her "Daddy." She and her Mother were both converted shortly after he found the Lord. The church they began attending was called "The Christian Church." Although her Dad was paralyzed and could not enter the baptismal for immersion, Lola and her mother were baptized together in this church.

GORDON'S STORY

Wintertime in Nebraska! Snow had settled in great drifts on the leeside of trees, fences and buildings. Christmas celebrations were over and New Year's Day was just around the corner. On Mom's day for baking bread, the process began by starting the yeast the night before and took much of her time and energy during baking day. Some time in the afternoon, the bread finally came out of the oven.

With the old-fashioned cook stove, she wasn't always certain how her bread would turn out. On this particular day, something besides baking bread happened. She didn't know how that would turn out either, but she named him Gordon—a name that has stuck for many long years!

Dad was a farmer. That means I was born in a farmhouse – the fifth boy in the family. No doubt that was a terrific disappointment to Mom, though it might have suggested more help in the future for Dad. What my older brothers thought about it is unknown. (That's probably just as well.) In those days, Dad was a rental farmer and had to share a portion of his crop with the landowner – one reason we moved quite often.

My first habitation was in a place called "the bottom." (Don't ask me why.) When I was about three years of age, we moved to the Russell Place.

Possibly only one distinct memory comes to me from my first home. Quite a few more memories can be recalled from the Russell Place. Among these were the mulberry orchard, where I gorged myself on mulberries and became very sick, and the cider barrel that blew up. (Apparently gas forms when cider is fermenting and something ignited the gas.)

Very early I had a penchant for running away. My mother used to tie both my brother and me to the clothesline to keep us from running away while she was hanging up the clothes. Once during harvest time, Dad took me with him when he was husking corn. I must have gotten bored with just hearing the "bang bang" of ears of corn hitting the wagon box. Somehow I figured out that we were near the public school. I slipped through the cornrows and wound up at school. No doubt, amongst other things, this greatly embarrassed my brothers.

During this period of my childhood in Nebraska, I have only three memories related to God and the church. The first happened on a hot summer day when my two older brothers were cultivating corn in a field near our home. My mother prepared a refreshing drink to serve to the boys when they came by with their team of horses and cultivator. We were gathered in the shade of a tree that stood near the edge of the cornfield. One of my siblings brought up the topic of angels. Mom taught us what she understood about angels. All I remember is that the idea of angels was completely new to me and sparked my curiosity. That was probably the summer of 1928.

That same summer brought about the second memory related to God and church. My parents were planning to move to North Dakota. They made a trip up there to make advance preparations for the move. My brother Leonard and I were left with our uncle and aunt while our parents were gone. We were with Uncle Harry and Aunt Olive over two Sundays. They went to church both of those Sundays. If my memory is correct, that was the only exposure I had to church during my first six years.

The third event took place in school – a small, white, one-room schoolhouse about a mile from our home. At one of the PTA programs, my brother and I sang the hymn, "Rock of Ages." The hymn had no meaning to me then but is worthy of mention because the public school played an important role in making me aware of Christ. Also, singing on this occasion was my first public performance.

During those early days in Nebraska, we were privileged to live near family. Grandma and Grandpa Bell lived up the road in one direction. Uncle Leonard and Aunt Bessie lived down the road in another direction. Uncle Harry and Aunt Olive lived not far way. An annual Christmas gathering at Grandma and Grandpa's house meant a chance to get together with all of the cousins. At one of these Christmas gatherings, my Dad arranged that his youngest son show off by standing up and reciting a poem – the beginning of my speaking career.

Soon after this, life was to change drastically. My grandfather had purchased some land from the railway – located eighteen miles northeast of Bowman, North Dakota. Dad decided to purchase this land from his parents. With no buildings on this land when we arrived in North Dakota, at first we lived on a rented farmstead about two miles away. Dad was so keen to be on his own property that he built temporary buildings as soon as he and we moved into this very unfurnished farmstead.

A barn with a straw roof brings vivid memories of milking with water dripping from the roof and sometimes down my neck. The house was a basement with basically an attic built over it. We lived in the basement and slept in the attic. Dad hoped to build a proper house on that foundation, but crop failures and dust-storm years made that impossible.

The nearest Methodist church was five miles to the west of us, holding services only during the summer months. As early as eight years of age I can remember praying, "God, show me your purpose for my life." I can't fully explain that since we were not a church-going family. Perhaps the Christian radio broadcasts mother listened to planted seeds.

Dad occasionally got in the mood to take his family to church. Shoes were patched, clothes made ready. The whole family went to church together in a 1928 Chevrolet truck. Dad, Mom and my little sister rode in the cab. We boys rode in the back of the open truck bed. To the best of my memory, we went to church probably not more than a dozen times prior to my seventeenth year. Even so, at this stage in my life, the Lord sent other wonderful influences into my life. On Sunday my mother listened to Christian radio broadcasts, such as, the Old Fashioned Revival Hour and the Heart To Heart Hour.

Secondly, a godly lady from the Methodist church became concerned for the boys and girls in the area who were not in Sunday school. She went about the neighborhood distributing a leaflet containing suggested Bible readings. My brother and I decided we would follow them. By means of the index, we looked up the suggested readings. As I read the Bible, God himself seemed to speak to me. I became aware that I was a sinner. At that stage I didn't learn what to do about it, but I felt an awareness of a deep need.

A third event that directed God's grace into my life occurred at our public school. At the end of the school year, our teacher for the upper classes found some Christian books and literature in our small school library. He took it upon himself to clean all of that stuff out and have it thrown away.

It was all dumped in a pile in the basement with the intent that it should be burned. My brother, one of the neighbor boys, and I pawed through that pile and gathered up several books, pamphlets and tracts which we put with our things and took home to read. Most of it was Moody Colporteur literature. (A colporteur is one who distributes literature – in this case Christian Literature.)

These books, pamphlets and tracts made excellent reading for my brother and me as we took turns sitting on the lonely prairie watching the cattle. Usually there was no human being in sight and nothing to do but watch cattle eat grass. That gave us plenty of time to read some of those Moody books. One of them was entitled "The Romance of a Country Doctor." My only memory about it is that some of the people in the story found a vital relationship with Christ that transformed their lives. An awareness grew that they had found something that was lacking in my life. Sitting alone in the deep silence and profound loneliness of the prairie gave the Lord opportunity to make His presence felt.

A fourth factor that strengthened all of this was watching the herd on Sunday afternoons. At that time neighbors from all around gathered at the schoolhouse for worship. How could a child suffering from loneliness and boredom keep from wondering what was happening inside the school-house, visible from where I sat. This too, sparked curiosity and some desire to find that good thing in their lives that was missing in mine.

Up to this point, my understanding had been that one just did the best he could and hoped that when he got to the pearly gates, Peter would say, "Come on in." Looming strongly in my mind was the question, "What if Peter tells me to go away?"

About this time, when I was fourteen years of age, a fifth important event took place that helped to answer that question. Mother listened regularly to a Christian radio broadcast called Sunday Vespers. The host of the program was Dr. Paul Scherer. At the close of one of his broadcasts, when I was fourteen years old, he answered a question sent in by a lady in his listening audience: "Can you know for certain in this life that you are going to heaven?"

This immediately caught my attention, since that was my great question. Dr. Scherer replied saying, "Yes, we can know for certain!" He quoted I John 1:9 – "If we confess our sins, he [Christ] is faithful and just to forgive us our sins and to cleanse us from all unrighteousness." He explained carefully and simply that God is not a liar. He keeps His promises. If we do our part, He will do his. Our part is to confess, sincerely from the heart, that we are sinners. That night by my bedside I knelt and confessed my sin and thanked the Lord for forgiving me. God spoke a deep peace to my heart.

There is no doubt in my mind about the importance of that event. To be quite honest, though, at that time there was very little change in my life. There was no family support for living the Christian life. Our family did not attend church. For that reason, I had very little Biblical knowledge for a foundation. Life on the farm followed the usual routine and several more years passed before the next important decision was made.

Some of that story follows.

THE BIG MOVE

Excitement was in the air. Dad brought home a brand-new 1928 Chevrolet truck—without doubt a very big event in the life of our family. He bought just the cab and chassis; with a plan to build his own wooden truck box. I have memories of the aroma of freshly sawed or planed wood as the carpentry work progressed. A canopy was fashioned to sit on top of the truck box. We were to have a motorized "covered wagon" in which to move.

My older brothers turned the crank to make the bellows roar. Forced air hissed through the charcoal in the forge, turning the coals into glowing red and blue. Pieces of iron placed in those hot coals soon became red hot. The hot irons were gripped with tongs and placed on the anvil where they could be hammered into shapes that formed brackets, clamps and fasteners needed for the construction. As a five-year-old, I was watching, smelling and listening. Curiosity led me to investigate. Amongst other things I found out that the anvil was very hot, even though it wasn't red like the iron from the fire.

When the project was completed, it provided the place where the five Bell brothers would ride on the move from Boone County, Nebraska, to Slope County, North Dakota. Grandpa came indoors with icicles on his mustache one morning in early February. The temperature was below zero. Our family had moved out of Russell Place the day before and bunked at my grandparents' house for the night.

Ears were tuned to the radio, listening for the weather report. Was it safe for a man to set out with the eight members of his family on this journey? Apparently it was deemed to be all right because we set out that morning, despite the frigid temperatures.

I remember some of the details about the trip. Quilts and blankets were laid on the bottom of the truck box to form a nice soft bed several inches deep. We five boys climbed in through the back door and lay down on the bedding. We could rise up on our elbows and look out the window from time to time. We could also sit up in the center where the arch of the canopy was highest. That made it possible to change our position from time to time. Dad made a window in the front of the canopy to correspond with the window in the back of the cab. In that way we could look forward and see the road ahead.

A small laundry stove stood in the right rear corner of the truck. It was placed at some distance from the bedding for safety reasons. No doubt it was bolted to the floor. A stove-pipe went out the top of the canopy. Charcoal briquettes were the main fuel, with corncobs to ignite them. My older brothers must have maintained a fire to keep the truck warm. I assume that the stove was dampered down most of the time, but especially when we were traveling.

At the end of the first day of travel, we stopped for the night. Mom and Dad took my sister Margaret and one of us boys (either Leonard or me) with them to the hotel. The rest put up for the night in the truck. I seem to recall that Mom fixed baloney and peanut butter sandwiches. Perhaps the laundry stove was used to heat some things. I don't remember eating in a restaurant.

The first day and night were uneventful. On the second day as we traveled northward, we ran into a blizzard. Sometime during the day, travel became unwise. Dad decided to park in the town of McLaughlin, South Dakota. McLaughlin was on the border of the two Dakotas. If the blizzard hadn't struck, we would probably have made it to our destination that night.

Blizzards in that country usually lasted three days. This one was typical, stranding us in McLaughlin for three days. One of the memories that stands out from those days was my first experience with Sioux Indians. Men, covering themselves with Indian blankets, appeared on the streets—a new sight for a small boy.

On the fourth morning, the wind had died down and the sun came out. We were delayed, however, until snowplows could open the roads. When finally we traveled north out of town, we found snow banks on either side of the road. The banks were so high that it seemed as if we were driving through a tunnel until we were out in the open country. There, nothing caused the drifting snow to settle in deep banks.

In order to complete the remainder of our journey in one day, we needed to travel approximately 140 miles. Road conditions made progress slow. In spite of the difficulties, we arrived after dark at the home of one of our new neighbors. They lived about two miles from our first new home in North Dakota. We stayed overnight at this neighbor's house and went on to our new home the next day.

Our new residence, called the Cole Place, would be home for us until Dad built housing for us on his own land. Mr. Cole, the owner, lived in the tiny town of Mineral Springs and operated a small grocery store. The income from that, along with rental of his land, provided a living for him and his family.

Now for a while, we had a substantial two-story farmhouse with several bedrooms, a living room, dining room and kitchen. In those days, indoor plumbing was lacking in almost all farm homes. The pump was in the front yard, not far from the kitchen door. Beside it was an abandoned well with a wooden cover. We boys found it interesting to peer through the cracks to see what was in the well. Fortunately, none of us fell in.

I remember quite clearly having frequent dreams about the house we left behind in Nebraska. I asked more than once, "When are we going back to our real home?"

The greatest challenge to me was adjustment to a new school. I had been in kindergarten back in Nebraska. My memories of that experience are very pleasant. Now I was thrust into first grade in the middle of the year. My teacher, not a happy person often said to us, "Behave yourself or I'll slap you to sleep." On occasion, she carried out her threat. Sometimes I was the victim. Most probably I deserved it, but I don't remember that part.

THE STRAWSTACK ADVENTURE

"Daddy, tell us another story about when you were a boy!" was an oft-repeated request by my own four little boys. The stories they knew by heart were the ones they wanted to hear over and over again. "Well, what story do you want me to tell this time?" I would ask. "Tell us the one about the strawstack," they would reply.

This event happened many years ago when I was a boy about eight years of age. Spring had been around for a while, spreading beauty and cheer .The snow had long since gone from the prairie. Meadowlarks had come with their cheerful songs and had not only nested, but had produced their first brood. Spring wheat had been planted, and by now the fields were verdant green. The last day of school was fast approaching. On this day, the sun shone brightly. School was out in early afternoon. Several of us were walking together, and the balmy weather gave all of us a sense of delight. The sun was still high in the sky, suggesting that there was time to have some fun and still get home before it was late.

Two neighbor children, Maynard and Laura Sowden, joined us as we walked home from school. They were about the same age as my brother Leonard and I. On their way home, they had to walk past our house. As we approached the gate to our driveway, I shouted to everyone, "Beat you to the strawstack!" (The strawstack was probably 25 feet in diameter at the base. It was probably one hundred yards from the entrance to our lane.)

Our strawstack had something unique about it. Amongst other things, I wanted my friends to come and see what it was. During the winter months, the horses had steadily eaten into the side of the strawstack. Instead of eating here and there at random around the stack, they burrowed a hole straight into its side. After several months, the horses created what seemed like small caves in the sides of the stack. Some caves might be as much as eight feet long, four to five feet high, and two to three feet wide. For some reason, after the horses were that far into the stack, instead of going straight they ate pockets to the right and to the left. This caused the cave to be shaped like a "T."

At my call, everybody raced toward the strawstack. I managed to get ahead of the others and ran around to the back side of the stack. The caves were on that side of the stack. My plan was to hide in one of them and see if the children would wonder what had happened to me. At full speed, I ran headlong into the far end of the cave. As I did so, I stumbled over something that moved and I fell into the opposite wing of the "T" from which this living thing was lying. It rose on its haunches and began making sounds that best can be described as "woof, woof."

I had just come into the cave from bright daylight. My eyes had not yet adjusted to the semi-darkness of the cave. I could not see what it was that angrily growled at me. Slowly as my eyes adjusted to the dim light, I could see two eyes gleaming at me. In the shadows, I could make out only the faint outlines of an animal sitting on its haunches and looking at me. I was scared out of my wits and my heart was pounding furiously. My mind pictured a wolf opposite me, trapping me inside its den. Would I get out of this alive?

After what seemed to me like an eternity, the others became aware that I was in serious trouble. Fortunately, my older brother William happened to be working close by. They called him, and he came to the entrance of the cave.

The "wolf" turned out to be a mother pig. She had found her way into the cave to make a nest in which to give birth to her piglets. My brother began talking to her calmly. When he thought that she was calmed down enough, he told me to move gingerly to the opening and get out. She "woofed" at me as I moved to go out, but gratefully did not grab at me or bite me.

I don't recall having any further adventure that afternoon. I, for one, had had my share for that day.

My brother put a barricade in front of the entrance of the cave to make it safe for the expectant mother to prepare for her brood. The next morning she had thirteen piglets. Had little pigs been there the afternoon before, I likely would have stepped on one and brought the full wrath of that protective mother upon me. Whenever I think of that event, I thank God for His protection on this and many other occasions in my life.

JIMMY

Every red-blooded child loves adventure. The story of my childhood would not be complete without some account of adventures with our horse Jimmy.

One of the summer assignments for the younger Bell boys was tending our father's herd of cattle. A half-mile from our farmstead was a square mile of virgin prairie land. The neighbor to the north of us rented the north half of that section. Dad rented the south half.

Rent from our pasture land went to support the public school. In fact, the school for that township was located on the southeast corner of the half that we rented. Because of a combination of the drought and the depression, Dad could not afford to buy fence for the pasture. That meant that we kids, primarily Warren, Leonard and I, spent many long, boring hours sitting on the hillside with very little to see, and most of the time with nothing happening.

Dad was concerned for our safety. Since his practice was to let a bull run with the cattle, he had reason to be concerned. Over the years, older bulls were exchanged for younger ones or for one of a different breed. When those bulls grew to maturity, they would weigh nearly 2,000 pounds. They could be mean-tempered at times and dangerous for an experienced adult, let alone young boys, to handle.

In order to make it somewhat safer, Dad put a ring in the bull's nose. When the hole in the nose became healed and healthy, he fastened a chain to the ring. If anything happened, we could grab the chain and possibly save ourselves. Another precaution was a pony for us to ride. When we were mounted on a pony, the bull was much less likely to charge. If we sensed danger, the pony could run fast enough to get away. Along with the pony, we always had a dog with us. It is quite possible that I would not be here to tell this story if it had not been for faithful dogs. The final safety equipment was a whip. Often a sharp crack of the whip would turn the bull away.

As mentioned before, we had the south half of a section of prairie land for our pasture. The neighbor who rented the north half of the school section built a fence around his pasture. Our cattle and his cattle could drift near the fence at the same time. The neighbor's bull ran with his herd, too. That made for potential trouble. We boys knew that the safest thing was not to let that happen. On the other hand, just imagine how time dragged on and how boring life could be out there on the prairie with no one in sight and nothing to do. Temptation would grow quite powerful. Here are some of the thoughts that made temptation grow. "I'll bet our bull is more powerful that their bull. Let's give them a try at it and see what happens." A little excitement would help time pass faster.

As the two Goliaths drew within two or three hundred yards of each other, they would begin to bellow and paw the ground. These mighty beasts could tear up a large chunk of sod with a sweep of their front hoof. The very ground almost seemed to shake as these champions challenged each other from a distance.

When things got this interesting, I might chicken out. If those two got to fighting, they might break the fence. Who knows how much trouble I would be in then? By calling the dog and riding at the bull with the whip cracking, I could usually get him to turn and then I could drive him away from the other herd. Then too, we might "sic" the dog on the neighbor's bull and get him to turn away. Most of the time, one or the other or both would work. A few times, a fight broke out, and the bulls went at each other through the fence. The ripple of those powerful muscles, especially in the neck and front shoulders, was an inspiring sight. The temptation to just let go and see which one would win did not last long, because the stakes were too high. Some way, with the dog's help and the use of the whip, the great animals would separate. We could then drive the bulls with their herds away from each other. What a relief when calm was restored and no great damage had been done. Nevertheless, the excitement of those events is still vivid in my mind.

One of our ponies was Maude, a gentle and well-trained horse. When I was about nine or ten years of age, Maude gave birth to a male colt. He was named Jimmy and became a beloved pet. He was gentle to be around, though very full of life. When Maude was running rapidly across the prairie, Jimmy would run circles around and around her. My dream had always been that Jimmy should not be turned into an old workhorse. I wanted him kept for a saddle horse. That was not to be, however, because he grew so large that Dad felt he was needed for heavy work. For that reason, it became my duty to use him in both roles. On his back, I had the most fun as well as some adventures that were a bit scary.

A hobby of mine was hunting and trapping. Sometimes I rode Jimmy to school. On the way, I would swing around to check my trap line. This particular morning, we rode over a fairly sharp rise. Just as we were starting to descend from the ridge, a skunk appeared in full arousal display. When Jimmy saw it, he spooked, grabbed the bit in his teeth, whirled around and took off at full speed. As he did this, he contracted his chest causing the saddle to become completely loose.

I was able to pull his head around enough to turn him the direction of the school. By carefully balancing the saddle so that it didn't roll to one side or the other, Jimmy and I arrived at the school together. Right at the barn door, he finally calmed down enough to respond to my pull on the reins and my call, "Whoa!" The saddle was still loose, making it necessary to carefully take both feet out of the stirrups, swing one leg over and slide off without turning the saddle. Wow! That was not only a fast ride to school, but also a dangerous one with the saddle so loose. After such excitement, my studies probably didn't fare very well that morning.

The next episode took place later that year. Winter had come and the crops were all out of the fields. This time of the year, free range was permitted. That meant that cattle and horses could roam freely in search of good grazing. Dad had let our horses run free to find the best feeding grounds they could. Often the horses did very well and became rolling fat. We were delighted to see them looking so well.

In order to keep track of them, someone had to ride out and hunt for them once a week – not only to see where they were but to also make sure they were doing well. Jimmy had been kept in the barn for riding purposes. A Saturday, with no school, was a good time to check on the whereabouts of the horses. It became my assignment to go and search for the wandering herd.

I threw the saddle on Jimmy and gave his chest a good bump with my knee to make him draw in his breath so that the cinch could be pulled up good and tight. I wanted no more wild rides like that one balancing the loose saddle. The weather was brisk. Jimmy was full of life as usual.

The horses had last been seen about two and one-half miles to the southeast. It made sense to strike out in that direction. If they had traveled from there, it probably would not be far in one direction or another. Jimmy did just fine. We made good time. On the way we passed the school and journeyed on another mile or more. Quite soon we found the horses. All of them were there. They seemed to be doing very well. With no good reason to delay, we turned toward home. That certainly suited Jimmy's mood.

Since we would go by the school, I decided to stop by and give a message to the teachers who resided in the "teacherage" just a few yards from the school. When that little errand was accomplished, they requested me to take home a quart jar and a gallon pail that had been used to carry hot lunch material to school during the week.

Let me say right here that it wasn't a good idea for me to agree to that. In fact it was a crazy idea to try something like that on Jimmy's back. Carefully, I tied the pail with the jar inside to the pommel of the saddle. When I proceeded to mount, the jar rattled inside of the tin pail. Jimmy took what seemed like a forty-foot leap. I missed the saddle but landed behind it with the reins in my hand. A ditch full of snow was beside the road. I pulled Jimmy's head so that he landed in the snow. That slowed him down. While he got out of the snow, I was able to get into the saddle.

On the way home, a little over a mile away, we had to climb a substantial hill. We made that stretch in what seemed like two minutes. I finally dropped the pail, with the jar in it, into the snow and pulled with all of my strength to get Jim slowed down. When we approached the gate to our driveway, I pulled him as close to the post on the right as I dared. At a right angle turn he was still going too fast for the circumstances. He slid on the ice in the driveway probably six or seven feet to the left but stopped short of the fence on the opposite side. Thank God, he didn't fall. We were soon at the barn door.

I make no boast for good judgment, wisdom or horse-manship. That was a crazy ride that should not have happened – like a lot of other crazy things I've done in my life. Jimmy stood at the barn door all in a lather. It was cold winter weather. I realized the situation could be serious. I put him in his stall, gave him a good rubdown and then covered him with a horse blanket. Apparently he suffered no serious consequences from the event.

Much more could be written about Jimmy, but I will not include more here.

THE DROUGHT YEARS

The building for Mineral Springs Consolidated School of District #18 sat on a section (square mile) of government land donated for public schools. To be very precise, it was located on the SW 1/4 of Section 15 in Slope County, North Dakota. One might say it was in the middle of nowhere. In fact, it can still be found on a North Dakota map about ten miles north of the town of Scranton. I went to school there for eleven and one-half years.

The day had started with beautiful sunshine and, after the morning chill burned off, was pleasantly warm. The younger siblings of the Bell family, Warren, Leonard, Gordon and Margaret, had gone to the school as usual. At noon, after eating our brown bag lunches, we happily went out to play. Sides were chosen and a vigorous game of softball went on. All too soon, the bell rang and we filed back to our seats.

We had settled down for the usual schedule of class recitations and study. In the early afternoon, a northwest wind came up that soon brought on an eerie semi-darkness, casting a gloom and pall over the classroom. The wind howled around the school building, whipping fine dust through the cracks around the windows. Even inside, enough dust was in the air to settle on the top of our desks and to make it irritating to breathe. Though somewhat unpleasant, escape from it was not possible. Enough light remained to continue with study and class recitations until school let out at four o'clock. We tied our handkerchiefs over our noses and mouths to keep from taking any more dust into our lungs than necessary.

Wind usually prevailed for three days before calm came again. Unless it rained, we would have another brown-out the next time the wind blew. And, my! It didn't rain for such a long time.

Dust storms were not the only consequences from a year without any rain. I was only in my early teens and did not fully understand everything, but enough was very evident. Our crops had failed, creating a lack of fodder for the live-stock that winter.

Dad had been working in the fields day after day in all that dust. On top of that, his worries about crop failure and financial loss made him sick. He was coughing a lot and complaining of pain in his side. One day that fall, clouds came in the sky. I can remember looking up into the clouds and praying, "Oh, God, please let it rain to settle the dust and help Dad feel better."

I had seldom been in church up to that stage in my life, but I did believe in God. I surely hoped that He would hear my prayer. (An old saying was, "They told me to cheer up – things could get worse. So I cheered up, and sure enough things got worse.") In fact, things did get worse instead of better. Evidently I did not have much faith that God would answer my prayer, and wasn't surprised that He did not.

Dad continued to cough. The pain in his side became almost unbearable. Finally, he went to the doctor. After a series of tests, he was diagnosed with tuberculosis. We couldn't believe it when the doctor said he must go away to a sanitarium for at least six months. Mom and probably my brother William drove Dad to a place called San Haven Located at Bottineau, North Dakota. Altogether Dad spent several years there.

Dad's being gone from our house brought drastic new adjustments in our way of life. At this stage, I was young enough that my mother and older brothers took the brunt of the responsibility. Life went on in spite of the difficulties. On the positive side, three of us, Warren, Leonard and I, earned our high school diplomas during this period. (William had completed high school earlier. He had gotten married and was out of our home by now.)

(This seems like a good place to note that Dad had become Chairman of the School Board. In that office, he negotiated with the County Superintendent of Schools a plan that enhanced the education available in our country school. By means of a combination of correspondence courses and what two teachers could teach, a pupil could earn a high school diploma. This diploma was certified by the county and the state, making it acceptable in many colleges. Quite a few young people graduated by this method. Since Dad had only an eighth grade education, I credit him with outstanding vision to work this out.)

Drought not only brought on dust storms, but through those years the grasshoppers multiplied by the billions. What the drought failed to destroy, the grasshoppers threatened to devour. During one of those blistering hot summers, Dad was out of the sanitarium for a while. The crops in the field had started, but for lack of moisture were stunted and about to dry up. Dad said, "Gordon, go with the horses and mower and cut down all of the wheat crop. We will cut and stack what we can salvage for hay." All day long the sky had been hazy. Not from high clouds, but from billions of grasshoppers in flight. I had been mowing most of the day and, towards evening, the grasshoppers began to fall out of the sky like hail. There appeared to be a dozen hoppers for every stalk of grain. One feared that they would devour everything.

The next day as the sun rose in the sky, a slight breeze came up lifting the grasshoppers like a mist off into the sky. They were in a migration mode and had eaten practically nothing during the night. How fortunate we were!

Dad was in and out of the sanitarium. When he was out, he would go back to working on the farm and his problem would return. Either during the second or third period of Dad's stay in the sanitarium, my oldest brother Oscar came down with TB and was assigned to the same sanitarium where Dad was. William was gone from our family home and Warren also wanted to leave. Farm life gave Leonard so much problem with hay fever that he joined the Civilian Conservation Corp (CCC's), leaving yours truly pretty much in charge of the farm work the last year or so. Warren was in and out to handle some things. Between him and Mom, I had help for planning and some of the work. My little sister Margaret helped at times by getting on her pony and taking the cows to pasture in the morning and bringing them home at night. (Fortunately, we had a fence around the pasture by this time.)

Nevertheless, sowing, cultivating the corn, putting up hay, cutting the grain and having it ready for threshing, and following the threshing crew from farm to farm pretty much fell on my shoulders. A day's work required rising very early to milk about ten cows and to feed the calves and hogs before breakfast.

Breakfast was over in a hurry. The horses were quickly harnessed to work in the fields until nearly sundown. Of course, the cows had to be milked again and the other chores done at night. Those were long, hard, tiring days. One blessing was that I could tumble into bed exhausted, but fall asleep immediately and wake refreshed and ready to go the next day. Certainly I had all the exercise needed to be trim and fit.

In the midst of that busy summer, the pastor of the Bowman Methodist Church planned to hold a Vacation Bible School at our little country church, five miles west of us. (It happened during a period when some time could be spared from the farm work.) My mother knew of my keen interest in the Bible. She agreed that, if I did the chores in the morning and evening for that one week, my sister Margaret and I could attend the Vacation Bible School. At the final session of VBS, the pastor gave an invitation to publicly accept Christ. There I knelt at the altar to fully surrender my life to Him.

Little did I know at the close of that VBS how soon and how drastically life would change for me. My older brothers took Mom to visit Dad at the sanitarium. While there, they made a decision that, since Dad's health would not permit him to return to farming and because none of the older boys wished to carry it on, they would sell the farm. Included in that plan was the decision that I should join a government program for boys called the CCC's. In September of 1940, I packed my things in an army-type foot locker and went off to live and work in Company 2772. This camp was in Roosevelt National Park located in the Badlands of North Dakota.

That last night at home shall always be sharp in my memory. To celebrate the event, I set a small strawstack ablaze. Obviously, I could never come back even to visit here again. My beloved horse Jimmy, and my dog named King, as well as other familiar animals and most of the things which had made up my environment, were to be sold at auction. For me, they would be gone forever. Even more devastating was the fact that family life would never be the same.

My childhood had given me very little experience outside of home. Not many jobs, even, had taken me away from home. Now, I was on my own and could never go back home to live again. A visit to home would be in a strange house and in very different circumstances. Admittedly, I had some attacks of nostalgia and some struggles to adjust to the new circumstances of life ahead.

No other professing Christians were in the camp, nor was it possible to get to church on Sunday. Any attempt to listen to a Christian radio broadcast would be quickly squelched. I placed a Gospel of John under my pillow. Waking before anyone else in the barracks, I read a chapter and prayed.

Even though I was a new Christian, I had a desire to witness to others of what Christ meant to me. What was said privately to individuals eventually was spread from one to the other. Finally one Saturday, boys came from all the different barracks and gathered around to give this religious boy a bad time. Needless to say, I had very little Biblical knowledge to help me handle that situation effectively. With the Lord's help, I held steady under the barrage. The Lord knew that his child needed encouragement and sent several of the boys around later to say, "Hang in there, Gordon. You are going the right way."

I entered the CCC's in September of 1940. The following spring, my eldest brother Oscar was released from the sanitarium and arranged to pick me up and take me to the Big Horn Valley in Montana.

POWDER RIVER BOB

One of the many good things about my summer in Montana was that my brother William lived there. William with his wife Lenoma lived in a little cabin in the Big Horn Valley. Their baby girl Sharon was just learning to walk. I hadn't paid much attention to babies up to this time in my life. Now I notice that this baby was as cute as she could be. At that particular time in his life, William was probably singing one of the popular songs of the day:

"Just Lenoma and me and baby make three, in my blue heaven."

In the spring, I found work in the beet fields. After the work in the beet fields was over, William took me around to some of the neighbors to find other work for me.

We drove into one farmer's yard and found a group of men gathered around a horse that had just been shod. They had thrown this horse on his side and tied his legs securely.

This was done in order to make sure that he would not kick them while horseshoes were nailed to his hoofs. After they untied his legs and permitted him to get to his feet, five or six men working together could not manage to get the rope off his neck.

In the midst of this scene, a pickup drove in. Out stepped a little bowlegged man wearing a cowboy hat. He stepped up to the group and offered to help. Soon he persuaded the men to turn the total project over to him. They let go of the rope, and he took charge. Looking the horse in the eye and talking gently, he slowly moved hand-over-hand up the rope until he was at the horse's head. Within just a very few minutes, he had set the horse free.

That was my introduction to Powder River Bob. When he learned that I was looking for work., he invited me to work on his ranch putting up hay for his cattle. I tossed my few belongings into his pickup and rode with him over the winding trail that led up to his ranch house. The road followed along Powder River as it meandered its way down the mountainside. I ate supper with Bob and his wife at the ranch house. Spending the night in a bunkhouse was a new experience for me.

The next morning he introduced me to the team of horses that would be my companions for several weeks. What a handsome team they were. One of them especially was a sight to behold. Standing in the bright light of the early morning sun was this gleaming white gelding with a graceful bow in his neck and a long, flowing mane. A sight I have never forgotten.

Bob helped me hitch the team to a mower. Behind the mower we attached a hay rake. The team, the mower and the rake were to take up my time and energy for the next several weeks. The ranch house we were now leaving behind us was already several miles up the mountain. I was to drive the team six or seven miles farther up.

At the beginning of the trail, Bob opened a gate into a small pasture. In this pasture he kept probably ten of his bulls. I found it a little intimidating to pass through that pasture with bulls all around me. Bob followed on horseback. He carried a bull whip and could turn away any bull that threatened trouble. He saw me safely through the gate on the opposite side of that small pasture and went with me to our destination. From that point on, the trip was quiet and peaceful.

Later in the day, we arrived at a small cabin. The Lord
and I were to be sole companions here for a good part of the
summer of 1941. Bob gave me instructions and left me with
food supplies. After that, he went on his way. Just outside
the cabin door was a flowing spring. The water was ice cold
and delicious. Washing my face in water dipped out of that
spring and taking a drink of that cold, delicious water was a
great way to wake up in the morning.

After nightfall, it was pleasant to sit on the steps of the
cabin and look up at the stars. At that altitude, the atmosphere
was unusually pure and clear. The stars seemed to twinkle
with exceptional brightness. The song writer's inspiration to
write these words from the song "Home on the Range" was
easy to understand.

"How often at night when the heavens are bright
With the light from the glittering stars
Have I stood there amazed and asked as I gazed
If their glory exceeds that of ours."

I slept at night with the windows open. On moon-lit
nights, I looked out the window to silhouettes of the mountain peaks. Through the open windows came a chorus of

coyote and wolf calls. A bit spooky —but I don't remember being particularly afraid. Admittedly, it could have been very lonely. The nearest human being was at the ranch house six or seven miles below, but the Lord was my close companion the entire time.

Every third or fourth day, I would wake up to find that Bob had come during the night. He knew the mountain trails by heart and did a lot of riding at night. One of the reasons for doing that was to keep cattle rustlers from driving away some of his herd. No doubt, one of his reasons for coming at this time was to see whether his hired man was on the job. Another reason was to replenish my fresh food supply. Amongst the things he brought was fresh lettuce. He would fix some for me. Sometimes he made a custard so that I could have a dessert for a change. Then he was off for another three or four days.

Bob was a legend in that part of the world. Some said that he built his own herd of more than five hundred head by rustling from other ranchers. Probably it was only partially true. He grew up around horses. He told me that when he was a kid, he slept in the manger next to horses. He learned the language of horses. He understood them and they fully trusted him. I saw firsthand that he had a special way with horses.

The ponies he rode across the range were all trained to travel with what he called a running walk. Trotting or galloping can be very tiring for the horse and for the rider. The running walk gave a smooth ride and enabled the horse to travel for hours at between four and five miles per hour.

Powder River Bob had an oil well on his ranch. One of his stories was about a man who tried to steal some equipment from the oil rig. Bob saw the thief load the stuff into his truck. Bob on his horse knew the trail well and took a shortcut. When the thief came around a bend in the road, Powder River Bob was waiting with his rifle in hand. The thief quickly returned the stolen goods.

I worked faithfully and managed to build some good-sized stacks of prairie hay for Bob's cattle that winter. When the job was done, I drove the team and the equipment back to the ranch house. I was delighted that he was pleased with my work and paid me well.

Such was the colorful background I had for entering college in September. I still value the special memories that summer gave me. I must admit that it did little to help me make the major social adjustments that college life would require of me.

TAYLOR UNIVERSITY

I have already written about the Vacation Bible School where I publicly accepted Christ. During that week of VBS, I discussed with Rev. Hutsinpiller my calling to the ministry. At that time and on several other occasions, he talked with me about a Christian college named Taylor University. At my request the college sent a prospectus. From this time forward I was determined to go to Taylor in order to prepare for the ministry.

Even before I left home, in September 1940, I was trying my best to save a little money to go to college. In the CCC's I was paid $30.00 per month. I often say that I earned $30 and saved $35. In addition to what the CCC's paid me, I stoked the fires in the barracks and waited on my table at the dining room. My barrack partners and tablemates paid me a little for these services. Wages were just a little better for the summer work I did in Montana. That helped me to save a little more for train fare and a down payment for the first semester of college.

When summer work was over, I rode the train from Hardin, Montana, to Clark, South Dakota. It was good to have a few days in Clark to visit my Mom and my sister. Boarding the train in little towns like Hardin, Montana, and

Clark, South Dakota, is a very different experience from arriving in Chicago. Pages could be written about my first impressions of Union Station. What a huge place! I didn't know there were that many people in the world. What should I do with my luggage? How could I find my way to the Salvation Army Hotel for a cheap room for the night? Would I miss my train the next morning from Chicago to Upland, Indiana?

Though this was intimidating, I managed to do what was necessary in Chicago. Boarding the correct train the next day, I arrived safely at Upland in early afternoon. Actually the conductor let me down beside the railway track. The only evidence of a station was a wooden signboard displaying the words, "UPLAND, INDIANA."

After finding directions, I walked more than half a mile to the college. I was carrying a large suitcase in one hand and a topcoat over my shoulder. When I arrived, I found my way around a little and was shown to my room in Swallow Robin Dormitory. After a night's rest, the first order of business was to see about employment. To my surprise they told me I was too small for farm work. (Too bad my dad didn't know that! What a lot of hard work it would have saved me.) I was assigned to work in the kitchen. That proved to be a good place for me to work. Some of my best friendships were made working side by side with classmates there.

Perhaps the most important thing that happened to me in my first year was being invited to participate in Student Volunteer prayer meetings. (Student Volunteers was an inter-denominational missionary organization.) These prayer meetings were held on behalf of missionaries serving on various fields around the world. Up to that time in my life, I had not been exposed to the idea of missions.

At the end of my freshman year, Student Volunteers chose me as a "sergeant at arms." In plain language my duties were arranging chairs, opening and closing windows and such janitorial chores. Apparently the society thought I did my job well. At the end of my sophomore year they elected me as president. From janitor to president – quite a promotion for me.

Student Volunteers had their monthly prayer meeting in an obscure room on the fourth floor of Taylor's administration building. The average attendance was a baker's dozen of committed students who believed in missions and wanted to pray for missions. To me it was important that the student body should have a greater exposure to missions than this.

In the course of the year that I was president, a number of prominent missionaries became available to speak at Taylor. I negotiated with the authorities to move Student Volunteer meetings from that obscure room on the fourth floor to a popular assembly room on the first floor. Again and again we had capacity crowds for special missionary services. By the end of that year more than a third of the class of '45 had committed their lives to service on various mission fields.

Up to that point, my only commitment as president had been for promoting the Student Volunteers organization on our campus. My attitude toward a missionary call remained somewhat skeptical. This is the way it appeared to me: A missionary would come and give an impassioned plea on behalf of Latin America. A number of young people would decide that they were called to be missionaries in Latin America. Another missionary would stir up peoples' feelings about the needs in Africa. Again there were those who said they were called to be missionaries in Africa.

At the end of my junior year, I was well into my philosophy major. I had studied logic. Emotions were not to be the ruling factor in my life. Reason must be the controlling principle governing my conduct. Emotional appeals were never going to determine my future.

The Lord knew how to get beyond that barrier. He brought to my attention certain facts about the land of India. One-fifth of the world's population lived in the sub-continent, but no missionary had come representing India's need. India's population was greater than that of Africa and Latin America combined. That India should be so poorly represented didn't seem fair to me.

After the Lord highlighted these facts for me, He directed my attention to the land of India in many different ways. Newspaper and magazine articles about India caught my attention. I became aware of students who had grown up in India and had parents who served there. Former graduates were veteran missionaries in that land. E. Stanley Jones, one of the truly great Christian leaders of that time, came and spoke to our student body. He was a missionary in India and had written books about that great land.

I began to wrestle with the question, "Lord, are you calling me to serve in India?" After much prayer and heart-searching, His will became clear and my calling was made sure. After a number of years the details were worked out. The course for much of the remainder of my life was now set.

EXTRACURRICULAR ACTIVITIES

During my freshman year, I came to know Wesley Arms. Through the years he has been a wonderful friend. Our professors had information from Ford Motor Company in Dearborn, Michigan, about summer work scholarships available. In June of 1942, Wesley and I went together to see what we could find. Wes found a room for us to rent. Both of us obtained employment at Ford's River Rouge plant, in Dearborn, Michigan. Dr. John Zoller was pastor of a gospel tabernacle in Detroit. His son John formerly graduated from Taylor. We decided to look up his tabernacle and ended up attending there for the summer. Zoller Gospel Tabernacle was the home of "America Back to God Broadcast." His rather large congregation included a lively youth group. Wes and I enjoyed attending the Sunday services and became active in the youth group as well.

Zoller's young people had a monthly outreach ministry to a rescue mission located on Third and Porter Streets in the heart of Detroit. I joined with the young people who had a part in that ministry. Among other young ladies in that group was Lola Kelley. Lola was an outgoing, friendly young lady. She welcomed new comers to young peoples' meetings and made people feel at home.

Youth meetings each week put us in touch with each other. We also traveled together on a streetcar to the mission meetings downtown. On one of these trips, I got up courage to ask for a date. She invited me to meet at her house for a meal and then have a game of tennis. Since the way to a man's heart is through his stomach, Lola baked a beautiful chocolate cake for dessert. When it came time for dessert, I begged off, saying that I was too full. After the game was over, we returned to the house for dessert. I was not hungry, even yet, for any of that wonderful cake. Lola worked hard to make that beautiful cake just for me. It is a wonder that our relationship survived my strange refusal of such a delectable morsel. (I failed to explain to her that very early in life I found chocolate brought on headaches. Apparently she never held it against me.) Soon after this it was time to go back to school.

Lola began her first year at Ft. Wayne Bible College and I returned to my second year at Taylor. During that first semester I went to Ft. Wayne to visit her – more than once. On one of those visits our budding relationship came to a sudden halt. We parted thinking it was over. Nearly a year went by without even any correspondence between us.

The summer following my sophomore year, I went back to my home town, Bowman, North Dakota. Providentially Rev. and Mrs. Hutsinpiller graciously took me into their home. During the summer I found various jobs that tended to be of short duration. For a while I drove a bread truck for Bowman Steam Bakery. Briefly I worked at the Red Owl Grocery Store. Eventually the Hutsinpillers were transferred. I was invited to fill the pulpit until the new pastor took over. That didn't pay me very much. I filled the pulpit on Sunday and worked on a farm during the week. A huge hailstorm completely wiped out the farmer's crops. The hailstorm ended my job on the farm. When the new pastor arrived, I was no longer needed at the church. It was time for me to go back to Detroit and try to earn a little more before school started in September.

My brother Leonard had come to Detroit and found a home with the D. M. Millers. Upon arriving in Detroit, I went to see my brother and the Millers. She graciously invited me to share Leonard's room at her house. Ford Motor Company compassionately hired me again, even though they must have known that my time would be short.

Being somewhat settled, I decided to give Lola a telephone call. A little to my surprise, she responded warmly.

Our friendship was renewed. In the few weeks before school started, we found opportunity to enjoy some pleasant activities together.

Mrs. Miller and Leonard attended Detroit Gospel Tabernacle. Because I had moved in with my brother at the Miller home, it seemed good for me to go to church with them. At that time, Lola worked at Michigan Central Railway Station as an elevator operator. Mrs. Miller invited Lola to join us for Sunday dinner. Lola came to church in the morning. We spent the afternoon together. That evening I went with her to Michigan Central Station. Opportunities such as these helped us to get to know each other better and know that we wished to continue our special friendship.

When I went back to Taylor, we had regular correspondence with each other. This was my junior year and the year that I acted as president of Student Volunteers on campus. Around November, Lola wrote that she was planning to come to Taylor for the second semester, beginning in January 1944. That was followed by my visit to Detroit at Christmas time. By this time I had become a student pastor and needed a car in order to pastor my churches. I drove that car to Detroit. In front of her house at 15158 DaCosta, she said "Yes" to my proposal in that automobile. We became engaged to be married.

With Lola on the campus, our visits were more regular. Among the pleasant things that began to happen was that we did things with other engaged couples. In some cases, married couples took us under their wings as well. This was a happy change of affairs for me. Admittedly, there was a change in my relationship to single students and to certain class activities. In the course of events, we set August 22, 1944 as the date for our wedding.

Taylor had no accommodations for married students. Student marriages were still frowned upon in those days. Mrs. Charles Schilling offered us an upstairs apartment in her home. All she asked in return was help to stoke her furnace and do odd jobs on the weekends for rent-free quarters. This seemed to be proof that two can live more cheaply than one!

My senior year was my best year academically. Both of us were going to classes and studying. We were happy and able to focus fully on our work. No doubt we paid a price for marriage at this stage. However, God has blessed us. We have only thankfulness for our years together.

PASTORAL MINISTRY AT TAYLOR

The year before Lola and I were married was a busy one. I had chosen a philosophy major. Dr. Ayers gave us difficult texts to study and practically required us to memorize them in order to do well on his exams. I was deeply involved in the Student Volunteer Movement. The Wabash Conference Superintendent of the Methodist Church had appointed me as student pastor of two churches – Griffin Chapel and Locust Chapel. These were located near Marion, Indiana. Rev. and Mrs. J. W. Holloway, a retired pastor and his wife, attended Griffin Chapel. They took me under their wing. Thank God for patient people who put up with a young fellow who had lots to learn. God graciously granted fruit even in those first years.

During the summer of 1944, I was transferred to Blackford and Oakland Methodist Churches, located east of Montpelier, Indiana. Later that summer, Lola and I were married. From that time on pastoral ministry was a team effort. In this second student pastorate, the Lord again graciously granted fruit. Young people gave their hearts to Christ during that year. One convert still writes to us. She married a fine Christian man and they founded a Christian home. Their children, grandchildren, and great-grandchildren have been brought up in the faith. The seed sown bears fruit generation after generation.

FOUNTAIN CITY, GORDON'S BABYHOOD

The order to move came soon after I graduated from Taylor University in June of 1945. The Indiana Conference of the Methodist church transferred us to Fountain City, Indiana, located about five miles north of Richmond, Indiana. Our new home was next door to the church. We also pastored Hopewell, a fine country church.

I enrolled in classes in Bonebrake Theological Seminary in Dayton, Ohio, for the summer quarter. Lola lived in the dormitory with me part of the time. On weekends, we carried out our duties in the pastorate. Most of the time she stayed at the parsonage to avoid the trip back and forth to Dayton. Summer quarter ended in early August. Our first son, Gordon Elvan was born on August 24. In late September, I was off to Asbury Seminary in Wilmore, Kentucky, for the fall quarter.

Caring for her own new baby for the first time was a bit scary for Lola. Fortunately, her Mom could come and that was a great blessing. Just to have her there for a few days was comforting and reassuring. Judy Cogshell, a young lady who lived close by, befriended us and was a good companion for Lola when I was gone. That too was a big help. Nevertheless, being apart so much was painful for both of us. I was gone from Monday afternoon to Friday. Weekends were busy with church affairs. Week after week of this routine was exhausting – almost impossible to do justice to anything. Studies, church and family were all short-changed.

My being away so much was doubly difficult because we missed each other terribly our first-born son was changing very rapidly. I was not home to help with his care or to enjoy him. At the end of that semester, I postponed my schoolwork and stayed home for the next year and a half.

We had given Gordon Elvan my first name. Having two people in the house with the same name can be confusing. For that reason, we began calling him G.E. G.E. would cry for his bottle and start his meal, but very quickly fall asleep. The doctor suggested that Lola snap the baby's feet to keep him awake. When she did this, he would awaken, take a little more milk, and go right back to sleep. G.E. just didn't seem to be hungry. Lola tried all kinds of tricks to entertain him and keep him awake so that he would eat. For example, the spoon became an airplane to make a dive into his mouth. (Lest the reader become concerned, G.E.

did grow up. On seeing him today, one would know that he survived quite well.)

On the other hand, as soon as we sat down to eat, he would awaken and cry. We learned to bring the buggy alongside the table. By putting a foot on the buggy wheel, we could rock him and manage to eat our meal in peace. He was the first of four sons who had trouble with colic. His tummy pains caused him to cry a lot. The doctor simply said, "He's practicing to become a preacher."

That first winter Lola took him to church regularly. She often had to lay him on his tummy on her lap and jiggle him while she patted his back. On one occasion, the jiggling started the whole church to shake a bit. The vibrations could be felt on the platform behind the pulpit. It was so noticeable that I stopped preaching and asked if it were an earthquake. The people smiled and pointed back to Lola and the baby.The next summer, when G.E. was more than nine months old, he would take his nap upstairs near my study. After we laid him down for a nap, he would make believe that he was sleeping. When he thought I was not watching, he would get up and stand by the side of the crib until he was laid down again.

That first summer on lovely, balmy days, Lola enjoyed taking him out in our backyard for his bath. That pleased him and he chattered so much that the neighbors knew it was G.E.'s bath time. That same summer he would walk beside me over to the I pulled the rope up and down to ring the church bell. Before long he began imitating my actions, as if he were helping ring the bell. At that age G.E. loved to stand beside Lola in a back pew and shake hands with the people as they left the service.

A coal stove at the center of the middle room of the parsonage provided our central heating. A coal bucket filled with briquettes stood beside the stove. G.E., moving past the coal bucket with his walker, couldn't resist the temptation to take briquettes out of the bucket and carry them over to the window ledge. When Lola scolded him for it, he would get a puzzled look on his face. He seemed to be asking himself, "How did Mommy find out that I was in the coal bucket?"church and stand watching while ff course his little black fingers were a dead giveaway.

LOLA'S MEMORIES OF LARRY'S BABYHOOD

Our second child was expected in early August, and arrived on August 9, 1946. We thought maybe this one might be a girl. That wasn't God's plan for us. G.E. got a little brother. G.E. was just eleven and a half months old when Lola came home from the hospital with Larry. G.E. rejected both of them at first. Soon he started loving Mommy again. Before long, he adjusted to having a little brother and learned to bring simple little things to help her with the baby.

Larry had digestive problems and cried a lot. The doctor changed the basis of his formula from diluted cow's milk to diluted Carnation canned milk. Thankfully, this helped the little fellow to do better.

My Mom was on hand again to help get Larry off to a good start. We were so grateful that she could be with us again.

Larry had a round face and looked very cute in a baby bonnet. When the time came, he took to solid foods very well. Soon his chest began to fill out so that we kiddingly said we should have named him Chester. Larry didn't start to walk until fourteen months. His learning to talk followed a similar pattern. We were a little worried until we were told that this was quite normal and nothing to worry about.

Before I move on to describe our time spent in Wilmore, Kentucky, I wish to highlight the fact that the pastorate in Fountain City, Indiana, gave us two years that were rich in learning and full of blessing. Two revival meetings resulted in young people giving their lives to the Lord. Some of those dear people were wonderfully supportive. Some became close friends. We look forward to seeing them in heaven

Our stay at Fountain City, Indiana, was from June of 1945 until June of 1947. Larry was about nine months old when we moved from Fountain City to Wilmore, Kentucky. He was using his walker quite a bit at that time. Household things were packed. Everything was ready to start on the journey to Wilmore. Just when we were about to leave the house for the car, Larry ran off the porch with his walker and landed in the mud. He wasn't hurt, but cleaning him up posed a slight problem because everything was packed. We managed somehow, and soon we were on our way.

On the trip to Wilmore, a tire blew out. We pulled over to the side of the road to change the tire. Gordon put a blanket up on the bank just a little above the road. I clearly remember that Larry played happily on the blanket in the warm sun. G.E. was probably watching his Dad and trying to be helpful.

Another episode in Larry's young life took place a few months later. He was walking now and exploring the out-doors with his "big" brother. He came crying to the house with his hand caught in a tin can. The lid had been pushed inward. Larry tried to pull out the lid and caught his thumb between the lid and the can. Any attempt to pull out his thumb only pinched his thumb tighter between the lid and the can. Since the lid was sharp, it was hurting him quite a bit. Fortunately the problem was quite easy for his Dad to solve.

When G.E. rode his tricycle, Larry loved to stand on the back, holding on to his big brother's shoulders. Most of the time the two little boys played nicely together. G.E.'s imagination usually found a variety of things for them to do, although sometimes his imagination led to some memorable escapades.

WILMORE, KENTUCKY

We moved from Fountain City, Indiana, to Wilmore, Kentucky, in the summer of 1947. My trying to continue Seminary training from Fountain City required a 200-mile trip each way. That on top of all the duties mentioned earlier had made it too difficult for me and I took a break for a while. We decided to move closer to the school and look to the Lord for guidance to make further training possible.

In Wilmore, I secured employment with the Southwestern Company. My job was house-to-house selling Bibles, Bible storybooks for children, a good dictionary and a few other books. Much of my work was in rural areas where people wanted the Bibles or books but could not pay cash for them. I accepted canned goods, sweet potatoes, and other farm produce in payment. It took all of the cash that came in to pay for the books and everyday living costs. We had food for our pantry, but no savings for going to school. Finally, after much prayer, we decided to do the winter and spring quarters by faith.

LOLA'S MEMORIES OF WESLEY'S BABYHOOD

Wesley was the only one of our sons born at home rather than in a hospital. There are, of course, special memories related to his birth event. Wesley came along in February during the coldest weather of the winter. Even in Wilmore, Kentucky the temperature could dip to below zero at that time of year. On top of that, the house was poorly insulated. Fortunately mother and baby suffered no consequences from the chilly temperatures.

Wesley was a healthy baby with a round face and dark short hair all over his head. He looked like a baby doll Lola remembers having when she was a girl. He was very easy to feed. Sometimes he drank two bottles at once and then slept for six hours.

For this third time in a little over three years, Mrs. Kelley came and helped for the first few days until Lola was able to carry on. Now with three little ones, life had become very busy for her.

LIFE IN LANSFORD, NORTH DAKOTA

The war had just recently ended. Manufacture of automobiles had been suspended for the war effort. Even used cars were high-priced and difficult to find. We succeeded in purchasing a nice looking 1941 Chevrolet in good condition (with funds borrowed from my brother Leonard). In that car we packed our belongings and our little family (now three little boys), to make the long journey from Wilmore to Detroit up through the Mackinaw Straights and on west to Lansford, North Dakota (about 1800 miles.) Lansford was a farming community with a population of about 300 at that time.

Wesley was between three and four months old when we left Wilmore to make the journey to Lansford. For the most part, Lola held Wesley in her arms as we traveled.

She remembers having a pillow between us to make a bed for Wesley. When she was too tired from holding him, she could lay him on the pillow and get a little rest. We broke our journey for a day or two at Lola's mother's home in Detroit before pushing on.

The second part of the journey took us through the Straits of Mackinac and west to Lansford, North Dakota. We had just enough money to buy gasoline for the journey. There really wasn't any extra for emergencies. (We both remember only having two dollars left in our pockets when we arrived.) Late on the second day of travel from Detroit, we arrived exhausted and somewhat dazed. The people had the cute, little parsonage ready and brought our first meal to us. After such an effort to get there, this was indeed a royal welcome. What a blessing! Larry had developed a fever and swollen glands along the way, but he quickly recovered. We were so thankful that he suffered no lasting consequences from illness on the trip.

The outer dimensions of our small parsonage were 20' x 20'. Downstairs was divided into a tiny dining room and an equally small front room. The kitchen was comparably tiny. Just inside the front door were steps leading upstairs. At the head of the stairs was a small study. To the left were two bedrooms with sharply sloping ceilings on one side of each room. North Dakota's harsh winters caused Lola to be cooped up in this small area for many long months.

A small basement made room for the furnace and coal bin. The furnace had a stoker as well as a thermostat. These were modern conveniences we had not experienced before. One register came up in the dining room, providing heat for the entire house. An opening in the ceiling above it allowed some heat to flow upstairs. Another first for us was a refrigerator. The house had no running water, but there was a cistern with a pump on the kitchen sink. This provided water for washing dishes and clothes. Water for drinking and cooking had to be purchased by the bucket. There were no wells in town and drinking water was hauled in by water wagon.

One of my first projects, in addition to pastoring three small, Methodist churches, was to repair the outhouse. The congregation provided supplies to make the repairs and hired an old man to help with the carpentry. Next, the cellar door was about to collapse inward and needed to be replaced. Thirdly, the church steeple gave signs of wanting to fall down. The old gentleman and I worked together to rebuild all of these.

Preparation for Sunday started Saturday evening. The coal furnace at the church had to be started up, so the church building could be heated and ready for service the next morning. Sunday mornings required a 9:30 to 10:30 service at Lansford. A second service convened in Maxbass, about 11 miles away, at 11 a.m. A third service took place in Russell, another 6 miles farther along, at 3:00 p.m. The total trip was 35 miles. I got home Sunday evenings between 5:00 and 6:00 p.m.

My salary was $100 per month plus parsonage. Along with the parsonage, the congregation supplied water for the cistern, coal for the furnace, and paid the utility bills. In addition there were occasional gifts of farm produce. Especially helpful was meat; when farmers butchered in the wintertime, they often brought us a ham or shoulder. Out of that salary came the cost of maintaining a car plus gasoline for the 35-mile trip every Sunday as well for visitation.

The Methodist pastor in Lansford had been the Boy Scoutmaster for many years. I followed in that tradition. Amongst the boys in my troop, two did their work well and were given a trip to the National Jamboree. One of those young men went on to enter the ministry. Raising money for the Scouts was just one of the many jobs assigned to the

Scoutmaster. Lansford had a town picnic and ball game to celebrate the Fourth of July. Boy Scouts took this opportunity to set up a hot dog and pop stand near the baseball diamond, with the proceeds going to finance the local Boy Scouts program. I helped the Scouts organize and carry on this event.

We thought our fourth child might arrive on the Fourth. Lola sat in the car near the hot dog stand and made herself as comfortable as possible. It was a rather hot day. Our boys played around and entertained themselves the best they could. We were all relieved when that event was over and the baby had not made an unexpected arrival. Lola was glad to go home and have me near enough to respond quickly if any signals came.

LOLA'S MEMORIES OF VERLE'S BABYHOOD

We didn't have to wait long! Our fourth son arrived two days later, on July 6, 1949, at a fine hospital in Minot, North Dakota, 30 miles south of Lansford. We were able to arrange for babysitters. Fortunately there was no need for a mad dash to the hospital. Everything went quite smoothly. Lola and the baby did well.

We remembered a young man in a previous pastorate named Verl. We decided to choose that name and put an 'e' after it. This is how Verle got his name. Lola appreciated her doctor's gentle care. On top of, that he charged virtually nothing for his services. She found out later that his name was Veryl. Lola wrote, "I was somewhat in shock to have a fourth baby boy so soon. I thought he looked very dignified and remarked, 'He might be president some day.' "

All the other boys had colic. To try to make it better for Verle, we bought Shelley brand bottles, in the hopes of making it easier for him to take his meals. Instead of colic for three months, he had colic for six months. He had enough trouble that between him and the other three boys, we lost a lot of sleep.

Just a few doors down from the parsonage lived the Ewers family. Their two teenaged daughters, Edith and Phyllis, loved to babysit our children. Although we could not afford to pay them any proper amount, they didn't complain. They loved to do it and didn't expect any pay. At least we hope that was true. What a blessing that was!

Four little boys! What bundles of energy they proved to be! They were all doing something at the same time. It was quite a challenge, taking care of the four of them while

Gordon was preaching. One Sunday I just gave up and carted them all home. Fortunately we lived just across the street. Sometimes people helped and sometimes not. Perhaps they were tired of it.

The older boys loved their baby brother and would bring things for him and rock his buggy when he was crying. G.E.'s active imagination kept both of us hopping. One of the things he did embarrassed us. He took a hammer and pounded on one of the doors upstairs. The door looked as if it had suffered smallpox. Fortunately it was not a valuable door.

Several members of the Lansford congregation were well-to-do. None of them lived in anything comparable to the "cute little" home they provided for the pastor. One member ran the town grocery store. Another operated the local variety store. Still another owned the lumberyard. A number of the farmers had large operations with expensive machinery and thousands of dollars in the bank.

I called several official board meetings for the purpose of discussing the possibility of building a new parsonage. Some of the members were for the idea and some were strongly against. After I would come home from a tense board meeting and tell Lola about it, neither of us could sleep for half the night. In fairness to them, one needs to keep in mind that these people had gone through some really hard times in the past. Prosperity was a recent happening. For that reason many still felt that they could not afford to build a new parsonage

What a triumph it was when the official board authorized me to start the fundraising. I made certain that the first donors pledged at least $500 each. For those who could afford to give that much, it was embarrassing to do less. In a few days the pledges amounted to $3,000. At that point I turned it over to board members to take it from there. They continued raising the money and, after we left, built a beautiful parsonage. Later still, they went on and built an attractive new church building.

Duane Ewers is one of the young people who stands out in our memories from the Lansford congregation. He was one of my Boy Scouts and went on to enter the ministry. Several people from the Maxbass congregation responded to the gospel. Gusty Fossum was the strong pillar of Maxbass congregation. Much could be written about her outstanding leadership. She had a daughter, Jean, who became a Christian when she was a young girl. Her growth in the Lord was beautiful to see during our two years on the circuit. I was honored that she decided to attend Taylor University, my alma mater. She went off to college in September 1950, and eventually became a pastor's wife. She also continued her studies, earning a doctorate and becoming a professor at Indiana University.

There was an unforgettable event with Jean's brother Chester. He knocked on the door of the parsonage quite early one morning. We invited him in, but he demurred, saying he wanted to talk with me privately in his car. He came right to the point and said he wanted to know how to accept Christ as his Savior. What a joy! Right there in the car he prayed and gave his heart to Christ. Chester became a faithful Christian, married a lovely Christian girl, and established a good Christian home. Later he was elected to the state senate.

Beth Carlson was another precious person we especially remember. She regularly came to Sunday worship, along with her family. On a number of occasions I visited in her home and had prayer with the family. Some years later, on a return visit, Beth told us that the Holy Spirit used our ministry to create a desire in her heart to know Christ. She accepted him a year or two after we left and was a faithful supporter of our mission work—corresponding with us right up until her death in 1995. Her daughter, Elaine, belonged to the Maxbass young people's group, became a staunch Christian, and reared a fine family.

Two short years and three congregations. What a joy to be used in various ways to be a blessing in people's lives.

Our congregation knew we were planning to go as missionaries to India. They held a farewell for us and we were ready to travel at the end of the month of May.

THE TRANSITION TO INDIA

The India Mission asked us to be in Ohio by early June. Before we left North Dakota and traveled east, we wanted to visit my parents and family members, who were now living in Seattle. May of that year was marked by having snow every day. On the 31st we drove to Minot in a light snowstorm to catch a train for Seattle.

The visit was brief but important for the older boys would remember their grandparents on my side of the family and have some exposure to their uncles, aunts and cousins. We wanted to show my loved ones that we cared for them. Our call to go as missionaries was something they didn't fully understand, so we felt it would be a mistake to complicate things further by failing to keep in touch with them.

We left our car in Minot and upon returning from Seattle picked it up and made the journey to Detroit. Lola's mother, Mrs. Kelley, made her vacant basement apartment available to us. We planned to live there briefly while details were worked out for going overseas.

CANDIDATE SCHOOL

Securing our spots as missionaries in India, however, took some time. We had been corresponded with officers of the India Mission for several years, in fact. They invited us to come to Candidate School at their headquarters in Elyria, Ohio in June 1950. Candidate School, as the name implies, was a week of classes and tests for new missionary candidates. The school gave us exposure to the language we would need to learn and to the new culture we would seek to adopt. Mission executives were given opportunity to evaluate us prospective missionaries. We knew before we went that the size of our family would be an obstacle for us.

A week or two following the school, we were told that we were not accepted. Our family size was the reason given. Now what should we do? We had resigned from the ministry. But we still felt strongly that the Lord was leading us to serve in India. For the time being, though, I had to find a way to support the family.

LIFE IN DETROIT, MICHIGAN

I started making the rounds in Detroit from one employment office to another. The River Rouge plant of Ford Motor

Company had my record on file from previous service during college years. They hired me. Wonderful! A paycheck was soon on the way. Unfortunately, within a few months Ford was planning a major reduction in personnel, and people with little seniority would be laid off first. My friendly foreman warned me to start looking elsewhere for employment.

Soon I was able to land a job at General Motors's Diesel Plant. By working two shifts, until Ford laid me off, I was able to catch up a little on our finances. Ford had been training me to do finish grinding. Diesel hired me for the same kind of work. The pressures were much greater and the new work environment rather distasteful. However, it did put food on the table and pay the rent. One advantage from a change of jobs was a shorter drive to work and a slight increase in wages.

MINISTRY AT STONE CHAPEL

During this period we were invited to minister at Stone Chapel, a non-denominational church in Farmington, Michigan. I usually worked the afternoon shift at Diesel, but sometimes I was required to work until midnight on Saturday. On those weekends, when there was little sleep, this bleary-eyed pastor was probably neither inspiring to see nor to listen to on Sunday mornings.

It turned out that the founders of this work were people who believed in "soul mating." This couple had left their own spouses and were living together because they were "soul mates." When I took a stand on this issue, the couple returned from Florida, closed the chapel, and sold the property.

Our stand on the issue helped some parents to rescue their young people from an unwholesome situation. All of those families sought other healthy churches, which they would wholeheartedly support.

HOPE RENEWED

Later that fall, Fred Tiessen, a leader from The India Mission, held a meeting in Detroit and stayed with us overnight. This gave us an opportunity to tell him that we felt strongly led by the Lord to be missionaries in India. Fred passed this word to the mission board in Elyria, who reconsidered our case and approved our appointment.

What a wonderful new turn of events! Though it was exciting, it was almost overwhelming - facing deputation in order to raise support and travel expenses for a family of six.

For several months I continued to work at Diesel and at the same time contacted churches for opportunities to speak. A number of invitations came. Life was very full with six days of work and meetings on weekends.

We were scheduled to sail on the Queen Elizabeth out of New York City on November 14, 1951. A great many things had to happen before then to make our departure possible. Included on these requirements was a summer deputation tour. I took leave from my job at Diesel Motors and traveled west.

GETTING READY TO GO

My deputation tour lasted from early June to early July. One of the memorable experiences of that summer was being camp missionary at a youth camp in North Dakota. Young people committed their lives to the Lord during the camp. At least one little girl answered the call to be a missionary. We had regular correspondence with her over the years until she finished her training and went to serve.

The Lord loves to give his children special gifts along the way. A friend from our former Maxbass congregation, Mr. Brown, wanted to make the trip to Seattle. He would provide the gasoline and the car if I would drive. A bargain hard to beat! I was given an unexpected chance to visit my parents and relatives one more time before going overseas. Then, as soon as I returned to Detroit, Cadillac Motors reinstated me and I worked there until our departure for India in November. What a blessing to have our needs supplied in that way!

The months from July until November were full to the brim with six days' work at the factory, meetings on some weekends, and putting together our equipment items from lists given to us by the mission. Acquiring everything on that list included ordering items of special equipment such as a pressure lantern and stove, an old-fashioned hand crank, washing machine and wringer. Crates and boxes needed to be built to fit some items. We purchased steel drums that could be sealed air tight for protection from water on the voyage.

During this busy time our four wonderful little boys needed and wanted time with their daddy, but he didn't have much time to spare. G.E. and Larry attended school that fall. Lola had to think about outfits for four boys to last for five years. They would grow every year and changing sizes had to be planned for. Clothing for Lola and me had to be thought of, too. She was a genius at that part of the planning. Shopping had to be done for shirts, pants, shoes, socks, underwear, and sweaters–everything we would need. Once purchased, all of the items must be packed for shipment.

THE FIRE

Amongst other things, I was involved in making repairs to Mrs. Kelley's house and rebuilding some things in her kitchen. Migraines, which had become a part of life since college days, slowed things down at times. Even though packing aggravated her allergies, Lola pressed on with the work in addition to housekeeping and care of her family.

Things moved steadily forward. By early November shopping and packing were nearly completed. When I quit my job at Detroit Diesel, our pastor Rev. Donald Dibble and his wife invited us to dinner in celebration of the occasion. After dinner, Lola and the children, as well as Mrs. Kelley continued to visit with Mrs. Dibble while the pastor and I went to hear Dr. Donald Barnhouse, a well-known Bible teacher. It was rather late when we returned home.

We were shocked to find a fire engine standing in front of the house with a fire hose pouring water inside and out of the house. A fire had broken out in Mrs. Kelley's home! The front door had been broken with a fire axe to allow the fireman access to put the fire out. There were three to four inches of water on the basement floor and things were a mess upstairs and down. When the firemen were sure that the fire was out, they boarded up the front door to make the house safe from intruders.

The Wilsons, our next-door neighbors, took us in that first night. The next day, Mrs. Kelley was invited to stay in her nephew's home until her house was repaired. Rev. and Mrs. Chalmers, pastor of Brightmoor Christian and Missionary Alliance Church, took Lola and me, along with Wesley and Verle into their home. One of Lola's dear friends took Gordon and Larry.

The steamer trunk with Lola's best dresses and my best suits, among other things, was nearly packed. Unfortunately the lid was open for last minute things and allowed smoke to permeat most of the items in that trunk. We were blessed to have good friends who ran a cleaning establishment and they volunteered to clean all of the badly smoked items.

We prepared a wooden box and carefully lined it with waterproof paper for packing books. When the books were snugly packed, the lid was tightly nailed down. That box was sitting over the basement drain in four inches of water. Since there was not time to unpack and repack, we simply moved the box out of the water and shipped it as it was. The books arrived in India without the slightest damage.

Two final paychecks came on the day of the fire. They were left on top of the dresser. The stubs on those checks were charred brown, but the checks were good and the bank cashed them. Praise God!

Mrs. Kelley's insurance agent was a personal friend. When the agent was notified about the fire, she sent adjustors who assessed the damage as a total loss. She was granted the maximum amount of her coverage. Within a week the carpenters were at work, not only restoring the house, but also making it better than it was before the fire.

We moved all of our belongings to a nice basement in the home of Rev. and Mrs. Chalmers. Before long we were back at packing again.

But there were more problems to come. G.E. came down with the flu. At the same time, he fell and injured himself so that he could hardly walk. Doubts rose about his being able to board ship on the appointed date.

Our '41 Chevy was badly in need of repair. In the midst of all of this, it stopped running. One of our dear friends called and said that this meant that we were not to go to India. Our answer was, "The Lord has burned bridges behind us. We have no choice but to go forward." By God's grace we boarded our train for New York, on schedule.

Two nights' accommodations had been made for us in a hotel near the water front. One of our memories of the day in New York was shopping at Macy's Department Store, where we purchased a set of Melmac dishes. Those dishes were our companions at meal times for several years.

The heavy luggage had been sent on ahead by a forwarding company with instructions to place it on board the Queen Elizabeth. When we boarded the ship, we immediately checked to see whether everything was there. To our dismay, the accordion had not been delivered. We called the forwarding company from the ship. They promised to get it there quickly and a man brought the accordion on board – just stepped back on the dock when sailors lifted the gangplank, and the tugboat began to pull the ship away from the dock. Whew, that was close!

G.E. had recovered from his ailments. Mrs. Kelley would soon be in her rebuilt house. We were together on board and could breathe a little easier at last. But not for long — as the tale of events

THE FIRST TRIP TO INDIA

Settling into our staterooms, finding our way around the ship and getting our bearings caused time to go by quickly. Soon we heard chimes calling us to dinner. We were guided to our assigned table, which was set with a pure white linen tablecloth, fine china and plenty of knives, forks and spoons. Our waiter looked sharp in his formal attire. With a polite half bow he asked, "My ay tyke ya awdah?" We may have heard or read that there was such a thing as a Cockney accent, but we had certainly never heard one. Lola focused on the word "tyke" and thought he was asking about the boys. After some attempt to tell the boys' ages, she caught on that he was asking us to give our order. He served us an excellent meal in pleasant surroundings.

We were assigned cabins well forward and by a porthole. The cabins were small and ventilation not especially good. Even though we had all of our smoky things cleaned after the fire, when we opened the steamer truck the tiny cabin smelled of smoke and cleaning fluid.

Traveling by ship went well until we crossed the Gulf Stream. Then our ship hit stormy weather and high seas. That first rough night, I had a vivid dream that the ship tipped forward so far that the water augers lifted completely out of the water and spun in the air. Then in my dream, the ship tipped backward and stood on the other end. Of course, it was not really that bad. However, it was bad enough. Our cabins were located so that we experienced all of the pitch and roll of the ship. The motion plus the smells soon made us all very seasick.

The ship's steward asked, "Do you want me to call the sister?" To Lola, sister meant a Catholic nun. She thought the only reason for calling a nun was for last rites. For that reason, she replied, "Oh no! Don't call the sister! (We later learned that sister is the British term for nurse.)

I came to the conclusion that staying with the seasick folk would help neither them nor myself. I needed to get well enough to help the others, so I dressed and found my way to the elevator. Traveling upward on the elevator in a ship that was rolling and pitching was quite an experience! In spite of intense nausea, I managed to make it to the top deck and out into fresh air. Joining others on the top deck, I walked vigorously in a wide circle. To my delight, the nausea soon cleared up completely. My appetite returned, and I was able to resume normal activity. Lola tried to make it to the top deck, but didn't make it. Nausea overcame her and she had to give up. She and the boys were seasick three of the five days on the Atlantic. What a wonderful feeling for them to step on terra firma when we landed at Southampton in England.

Customs formalities were a new thing to us, but the officers were courteous and helpful. We had been instructed by our friends at mission headquarters to trans-ship all of the heavy luggage directly to our port of departure. That saved us from processing all of that through customs in England. David C. Cook and Company handled that procedure, provided us British currency, and guided us to catch the train to London.

Soon enough, we alighted from the train and found what the British call a taxi. Their design and performance seemed old and quaint compared to the American cars we had left behind. We were glad that the driver knew how to find 10 Finchley Road–the address of the House of Rest, where we were assigned to stay while awaiting our next ship to sail.

The lady in charge sent us immediately to our room on the second floor. To our surprise, we found the room so cold that we could see our breath. Lola remarked, "Didn't they know we were coming?" Looking around, we found a gas heater. By putting a shilling into the slot and turning the knob – presto –there was heat. That was encouraging, but not for long. The shilling lasted only a few minutes and then another shilling was required to keep it going. We soon concluded that it was cheaper to crawl under the covers to stay warm.

They rang the bell for dinner at 7:00 p.m. Finding our way to the first floor, we followed our noses to the dining room. For the most part, the room was well lighted and attractive. To our dismay, the soup was mostly water with a few tiny onions floating on top. Boys with healthy appetites, who were starved by seasickness, were still starved when the meal was over. England was clearly still recovering from the Second World War.

Snow had blanketed the countryside from the time we left Detroit until we boarded the Queen Elizabeth in New York. Rolling green hills greeted us from the train windows on our way to London, but heavy fog with its depressive darkness draped over us like a wet blanket in the city. In the gloomy atmosphere, we set out to explore the streets near 10 Finchley Road. Finding an attractive little shop with some tasty morsels to eat was like passing through a gate into Alice's wonderland. Snacks were expensive, but we were able to buy enough to help supplement the meager fare at the House of Rest.

We shed few tears upon leaving the House of Rest and gloomy London. Our ship, The Strathnaver, was waiting at

Tilbury Docks when our train arrived. Immigration formalities for leaving England were more simple that those upon arrival. We were soon on board this second passenger liner for the final leg of our journey.

The Strathnaver proved to be quite different from the Queen Elizabeth. The latter ship, operated by the Cunard Line, was a very large ship with glassed-in decks that made heating and air conditioning possible. The Peninsula and Oriental Steamship Company operated the former. Their ships, popularly called P&O boats, were considerably smaller with all decks open to the ocean air. P&O boats usually made longer voyages. Their equipment and personnel were set up to facilitate such needs.

The open decks permitted the passengers to enjoy fresh air and exercise. We soon learned about games such as deck quoits. The plan and rules for that game resembles volleyball. Since a volleyball would bounce over the rail into the ocean, rubber rings were used instead. These rings could be used for other games as well, such as shuffleboard and ring toss. Playing games helped to pass the time and gave us the exercise we needed.

The first two days out were rather chilly on deck, but soon we entered through the Straits of Gibraltar into the

Mediterranean, where the weather turned sunny and warmer. The ship's officers and personnel changed from woolen uniforms to white cotton uniforms. To promenade the decks was now a pleasant experience.

LOLA'S VIEW OF TRAVEL ON A P&O BOAT

I was mother of four little boys from two years of age to seven. The open decks were nice, from the standpoint of fresh air and the fun of looking through or over the rails at the waves and flying fish. On the other hand, little boys like to climb. The thought of one of them climbing over the rail and falling into the ocean was enough to give me nightmares.

These British ships had an interesting way to help us start the day. Our cabin stewards were Goanese (Indians who came from a province in India named Goa). These stewards woke us at about six in the morning with what they called chota (first breakfast). On the first morning out, I heard a knock at the door. Supposing it was the boys from the other cabin and getting out of bed in my nightgown, I went and opened the door. To my surprise, this Goanese gentleman came marching in with a breakfast tray. I quickly ducked behind the door until he retreated.

Daily routine consisted of five meals per day – chota, breakfast, lunch, teatime and dinner. All six of us paraded to the dining room for the four times. After dinner in the dining room, we could go to another room for coffee and cheese to finish off our final meal.

In between meals, the boys enjoyed the nursery, giving Gordon and me some free time. A laundry room was provided for passengers on a deck in the rear of the ship. The laundry room was directly above the engine room. The noises from the engine combined with the noisy washing machines were not pleasant. The ship's propellers were just below, which caused vibrations and rattles. This, combined with fumes in the laundry room and added to the fact that I was usually somewhat seasick, made doing the family wash a somewhat unpleasant task. Gordon helped me some with the task.

STOPS ALONG THE WAY

The Strathnaver stopped at Algiers in North Africa. We had several hours here, giving us our first glimpse of a culture similar to the one we would find in India. Small shops with their fronts wide open to the street fascinated us. In Algiers, we took a course in Bargaining 101. We learned that there was bargaining for almost everything and that the asking price was probably at least double the proper sale price. I thought I made a successful bargain for a bottle of perfume. The man started at five dollars. He finally came down to twenty-five cents. It turned out I paid for a bottle of water.

Journeying on to the eastern end of the Mediterranean, we came to Port Said at the entrance of the Suez Canal. Without leaving the ship, passengers were able to bargain with merchants who came alongside with their goods in small boats. Leather goods, certain types of small furniture, costume jewelry and the like could be tied to ropes and sent up to people on deck. When a bargain was struck, money could be passed down in a pouch fastened to the same rope. A number of merchants in various small boats carried on this kind of trade with a fair amount of success. This was probably the sole means of livelihood for those individuals.

From Port Said, we proceeded southward through the Suez Canal with Arabia on our left and Egypt on our right. In the narrow and somewhat shallow Canal, the ship reduced its speed; hence traversing the 103 miles of the Canal was rather tiresome. Even in December, the sun was hot in the daytime. Fortunately, the nights were cool enough for us to sleep comfortably in our cabins.

The Red Sea was wider and deeper, making full speed ahead possible. One of the compensations during our time in the Suez, was the ability to view historical sights on both sides of the ship, some of which were mentioned in the Bible. At the southern end of the Red Sea, just after entering the Indian Ocean, the Strathnaver stopped at the Port of Aden. Aden had a population of nearly one hundred thousand. Our view from the ship was bleak and barren. One wondered how any people could live there, let alone such a large population. The Strathnaver took on water and supplies at Arden. No doubt both of these had to be brought to Aden by cargo ships from other less barren lands under British control at that time. British personnel on board did an excellent job of keeping passengers entertained and relatively content. Games, snacks between meals, and other forms of entertainment helped pass the time at the Port of Aden as well as all along the way. Everyone was relieved when the stop at Aden was over and we resumed our journey toward Bombay.

After two weeks of bobbing and swaying on the water, we had developed what is commonly called "sea legs." We went to our bunks on the night of December 9 still rocking and rolling to the rhythm of the ocean. I awoke around 4:00 a.m. on December 10 with a feeling that something was different. After rousing a little more, I sensed that the ship was completely steady. Reason told me that we were docked in Bombay Harbor. Excitedly I dressed and hurriedly went to the deck, eager to see and learn everything possible.

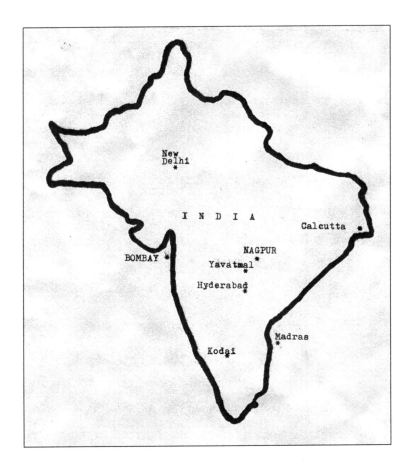

FIRST IMPRESSIONS OF INDIA

My first impressions were of people swarming like ants all over the place. Numerous porters (called them coolies in India) were dressed in drab, reddish-colored uniforms with red turbans wrapped around their heads. Very large and heavy items from the ship's hold were transferred from ship to dock by huge cranes, but anything small enough to be carried by a man or men was left to the coolies. We learned later that this was a humanitarian gesture to give employment to as many people as possible.

We not only encountered strange sights, but also new sounds and smells. Someone who visited India came back saying, "India is a land of bells, yells and smells." That says it in as few words as possible. A little later, Lola and the boys were awake and eager to take in some of the new scenes before us. Then it was time to pack up our small luggage and have a good breakfast before leaving the ship. That was important, because until we were safely at a hotel and could enjoy a good meal, stressful times were ahead.

The first hurdle on land was immigration formalities. Now for the first time we had to face processing all of our heavy luggage, along with the smaller personal baggage from our cabins. Our belongings were lined up on the dock.

While Lola and the boys waited patiently (or otherwise), I dealt with the custom official.

We were assigned an Indian representative from the American Express Company. He advised us that the custom official wanted a gift; otherwise he would require us to open all of our baggage. I told the officer that I would open the boxes, trunks and drums one-by-one, as he required. Just as I was about to unlock the first large item, a very tall British officer approached the custom official and said, "Let them through; they don't have anything you need to look at." Wow! What a relief that was. It was the Lord's doing and marvelous to us.

As soon as we were able to cross the custom barrier, we met Rev. Bill Tarter, who had come to meet us and help us find our way in this new land. What a blessing that was! He guided us through almost all that needed to be done until we boarded the train. Heavy luggage was carted directly to the railway station and booked for travel on our train the next day. A taxi was called and directed to take us and our small baggage to the Red Shield Hotel.

The Red Shield Hotel was part of the Salvation Army ministry in Bombay. Their accommodations and meals were modest, but for the most part satisfactory for missionaries.

Rooms were reasonably clean, beds more or less free of bedbugs, and western-style meals with safe water to drink were provided.

Here are some of the things that immediately impressed us. Large windows were wide open, day and night. There were no screens on the windows. We almost felt as if we were outside. Birds could flit in and out. Small salamanders crept along on the walls and the ceiling. The antique wooden furniture was finished with very dark stain and looked very old.

We noticed a number of things in the dining room. Tables were set with white tablecloths, substantial china and cutlery — no lack there. Chicken eggs were so small they seemed like bird's eggs, compared to Leghorn and Rhode Island Red eggs in the States. All in all, we were hungry enough that the food was edible and we had enough to eat.

The air was fresh in our bedrooms. Noise was not extreme, and the lack of swinging, swaying motion helped us to sleep quite well that first night. We arose early and spent some time looking out our window before breakfast. We were fascinated as we leaned out the open windows and looked down at the street below. For the first time in our lives, we saw people sleeping on the sidewalk. As dawn began to break, these sidewalk dwellers got up from their hard beds and walked away. Our third son Wesley was very impressed by this. He remarked, "These people just get up and walk away."

What impressed Wesley and all of us was that these people had no house keys, no door to lock, no possessions to leave behind, nor any real estate to mark a place that could be identified as home. Any little problems we might have seemed trivial by comparison.

The second day in Bombay had its share of business matters for me to tend to. Dollars brought in by travelers checks must be cashed at the American Express Bank. An account needed to be opened on our behalf to receive funds from abroad. I also needed to exchange enough dollars into rupees for paying bills and making purchases in India.

Our train was to leave from Victoria Station early in the night. For that reason, we went to the station dining room for our evening meal. We wanted to finish our meal early enough so that there would be no pressure of time finding our train, the proper compartment on that train, and the particular berths assigned to us. Bill Tarter helped with all of this.

While my mind was on other details, Lola was noticing different customs of the people. She observed the way people gestured with their hands, the signals sent by nodding or shaking the head, and others. At the table in the station dining room, we asked the waiter if this or that item was available. Instead of saying, "Yes" or nodding his head as we expected, he shook his head sideways from shoulder to shoulder. We thought he was saying, "No. We don't have that." After trying most of the items and getting the same response, we decided that he must be saying "Yes."

Victoria is a large station through which perhaps a half million passengers pass daily. As many as ten or twelve passenger trains may stand side-by-side in the passenger terminal. British rule in India made the English language popular. For that reason, it was not difficult to read the notices and find the correct platform to board our train. A passenger list was posted on that platform giving the carriage number and particular bunks assigned to our family.

Bill Tarter helped us to deal with coolies to cart our luggage to the platform and make sure it was put on board our train. In due time, all of the details were taken care of and we were in our places as the train pulled out of Bombay on its way to Hyderabad City, capital of the Nizam State.

How thankful we were for our bedrolls when we made up our bunks for the night.

During the dark of the night, our train passed through the coastal mountain range known as the Western Ghats. When daylight came, we were in the eastern foothills nearing the plains of Central India. How exciting it was to see the moving panorama that passed by our windows. India's vast population was not swarming over the countryside. Farms and pasturelands had a few farmers or shepherds here and there doing their work. Only the towns and cities swarmed with wall-to-wall people. Trees and vegetation of all kinds were new to our eyes. It would take time for us to learn the names and uses for many, many things.

Frequent stops at villages and small cities exposed us to new sights and sounds. The language, for the most part, was gibberish to our ears. A very few things were understandable. Hawkers called out, "Kawphee! Kawphee!" We soon learned that they were selling coffee. To our delight, bananas were on sale at every stop. Bill told us that we could eat the bananas if we were careful in peeling them – making sure not to touch the inside with our hands. He warned us that unboiled water was so unsafe that we dare not even use it to brush our teeth, even if we spit it out. In Bombay we bought makings for lunches, and canteens to be filled with boiled water for drinking along the way.

We arrived at Hyderabad City in early afternoon of the day after leaving Bombay. Somewhat to our surprise, Hyderabad was an independent state. Our experience was similar to crossing the border into another country. Customs were not as difficult as they were in Bombay. Other missionaries were there to help us through these formalities and take us on our way to our new home in Trimulgherry.

The India Mission had secured a vacated campus of the British Wesleyan Church. Included in our setup was a large central bungalow, as well as other buildings that provided quarters for several missionaries. Our apartment consisted of quite a spacious front room with an adjoining dining room. Just off the dining room was a kitchen. There were bedrooms for some of us, but two of the boys bunked in the front room.

The bathroom was in an enclosed veranda, a few steps outside our front room door. The toilet had to be flushed by pouring water from a bucket. Water for flushing, washing hands and showering was stored in a large earthen barrel conveniently located in the bathroom. While there were some adjustments for us to make, we were very pleased with the accommodations provided for us.

December was a wonderful time to arrive because the weather was perfect. Sunny days and cool nights could not be improved upon. Once I remarked to an old timer, "What a beautiful day this is!" His response was, "Nobody ever talks about the weather here, for one perfect day follows another." Enough said about the weather for now.

The Whitimores, missionaries who resided in the big bungalow, invited us to "cater" with them. We faced getting four boys, as well as ourselves, ready to trot up the street four times a day. (Teatime is a fixed habit in India.) This required sacrificing important intimate times with our family around the meal table. Lola wished to plan for her own family, which we did as soon as house help and other preparations were made. Undoubtedly this was a relief to the Whitimores, who had so graciously invited us to have our meals with them.

One of the concerns was whether Lola could manage all of the household duties and still find time for language study. This was a legitimate concern, and in fact, did make it very hard for Lola to complete her language courses. Trimulgherry had another disadvantage in this regard.

The people around us were either English-speaking missionaries or Indian people who preferred to speak

English. On numerous occasions, I attempted to use Telugu in speaking with local merchants. Very often they would respond by saying that they didn't understand Telugu, would we please speak to them in English. At times, I could ride my bike out to a village and find Telugu-speaking people who would listen. Lola was more handicapped in that way, since it was more difficult for her to get away because of the children.

Some of the younger missionaries were stationed at Bhongir. Boy and girls at Bhongir Bible School loved to have the new missionaries practice speaking Telugu with them. They were not hesitant to make suggestions of a better choice of words or simply to tell them that Indian people didn't speak that way. This was an excellent setting for learning a new language. We did not have this advantage.

There was no favoritism shown in placing people in one place or another and each location had its benefits. Trimulgherry had the best accommodations for missionary couples with families, while Bhongir was best equipped for single, language students.

BOARDING SCHOOL

Almost immediately, along with getting started with language study, we needed to make preparations to send G.E. and Larry to boarding school. We were warned before we left America that we would have to do this, but now we were face-to-face with the reality.

G.E. and Larry went to Breeks School located in Ootacamund, a town in the Palni Hills of South India... about a thousand miles away. Breeks was a British school and required both boys and girls to wear uniforms. Boys wore shirts and shorts made of khaki cloth. Along with these, knee-length woolen stockings were required. We had to purchase the cloth and hire tailors to cut and sew the clothes, as well as supplying woolen yarn to be knit into stockings. Lola had to sew nametags on every item of clothing–a daunting task. In addition, all of the supplies for schoolboys away from home needed to be bought for them. Some of these would be pencils, pens, notebooks, slate, soap, a soapbox, and a toothbrush. The reader can only imagine the stress on new missionaries in a strange land, adjusting to many things and facing learning a new language. On top of all this, think of sending two beloved children a thousand miles away to be cared for in a strange place and by people they have never met. Without doubt, this was the hardest thing we had ever done, and it was doubly hard for Lola. (One of the young mothers in our group of new missionaries broke under the strain. Eventually the couple had to take their son and return to America, where her health was restored.)

In less than a month after our arrival in Trimulgherry, we joined other parents who gathered at the train station to see their children off to school. G.E. and Larry would travel with other missionary children who had become their friends. Even so, when parting time came, it was heart-wrenching for the boys and for us. We would not see them again until mid-April, when we went to the hills to escape the sweltering heat of the plains.

Two missionaries went along as escorts for a group of more than a dozen children. These missionaries would see that the children were fed, avoided accidents, made transfer from one railway line to another in Madras, and arrived safely at school. Engaging coolies, arranging for carting and seeing that the luggage was transferred from one station to another was a huge part of the escorts' important responsibilities.

LANGUAGE SCHOOL

Wesley and Verle stayed with us. This was comforting, especially to Lola. Soon we settled down to daily routine, which included language study. We had one-on-one classes with a Brahmin instructor in the morning and the same with a Christian national in the afternoon – Monday through Friday. A minimum of two hours of study for each class was required. Annual exams took place in early November, giving us ten months to prepare for our first-year exams.

Learning completely new symbols for an alphabet was the first hurdle. Telugu has a few more letters in its alphabet than English does. By using a larger number of letters, the Sanscrit scholars had devised a way to express every spoken sound. The beauty of this phoenetic alphabet was that we could pronounce words correctly from the beginning, even when we had no idea what they meant. This was especially helpful for singing. Words are pronounced more slowly when sung, making it possible for us to more quickly join the Indian people in singing. Telugu has a relatively simple grammatical plan, which made learning the standard language a little easier than some other languages for now.

Learning a language is a laborious, time-consuming task. Over a period of months, it can become tedious, boring and even nerve-wracking. Senior missionaries who were in charge of our station encouraged us to participate in sports, outings and other activities to take our minds off the heavy grind and frustrations involved in language study. That's enough about language study for now.

One of the things we eagerly anticipated more than any other was letters from G.E. and Larry each week. This also meant that we wrote to them each week. The next most-looked-for event was letters from home. Regular mail took three months to arrive. An exchange of thoughts by mail took six months. We could send a letter by airmail, which we did some, but our budget did not permit us to send all correspondence by airmail.

Mail in those days was not entirely dependable. We actually saw postmen getting together and looking over each other's mail. Some mail was never delivered. On more than one occasion, we paid customs on gift parcels from America only to be given an empty cardboard box. Grandma Bell sent sweaters for each of the boys. One of the sweaters was removed from the box. Grandpa Bell sent watches that he had repaired. We paid customs for the box, but the watches were missing. Over the years, the standards of the postal department steadily improved, for which we were very grateful.

In the evenings, many of us gathered at the volleyball or badminton court. Vigorous activity gave release from tensions and presented a good opportunity for fellowship with others on the compound. Lola was often taken up with the two younger boys and household duties, missing out on these activities. Wednesday night prayer meetings, as well as Sunday services, also were enjoyable. From time to time, various mission programs took us off the station and exposed us to real-life issues in this new land.

One of the most pleasant experiences was making new missionary friends and beginning to get acquainted with Indian people. Then too, married couples enjoyed watching the young singles begin friendships that later blossomed into courtship and marriage. Some of our very deepest friendships were developed during the two years of language study.

In our December letter of 1952 we wrote as follows:

"We would like to mention a few of the things we have been able to do in addition to language study. Lola has taught Sunday school lessons in Telugu for the past seven Sundays. Gordon has preached twenty different times in English. For several weeks before exams, he went to the surrounding villages and preached in simple Telugu to the people. Almost daily the people come to our door for help. We often give them food and speak to them about Christ, sending them away with a tract to read. Thus, in various ways, we have had some opportunity to witness to the people even during language study."

HILL SEASON

This is from our letter of July 1952:

"We left for the hills on April 12. It took us three long, hard days and half of another to travel six hundred miles by auto. (Floyd Colwell tried to put his Model A in excellent condition before he brought it to India. New parts were not always available in the U.S. for a car that old. For that reason, it developed several major problems along the way. In addition, worn shoes from the feet of oxen were flipped upright by the front tires so that they were standing when hit by the rear ties. These shoes, worn thin and razor sharp, cut right through the tire and caused numerous punctures along the way.)

The first day out, the drive shaft pulley broke. Without the pulley, the fan belt didn't run. That left the car without water pump to circulate the water in the radiator and without fan to force cooling air through the radiator – a difficult situation anywhere, but impossible in India.

We had special prayer. Then Floyd started up this car to see how far we could go this way. His radiator was new and the engine clean. To our amazement, the car ran well at a slow speed. As we traveled slowly along, we began to pray that the Lord would help us find a pulley in the first village we came to. After about an hour, we came to a filling station (petrol pump) at the edge of a village. Floyd and I went in to see what we could find. Almost immediately, we saw on the wall before us the original Ford part that was not available in the U.S. What a cause for praise and rejoicing!

Answered prayer was wonderful and very encouraging. We were still faced with many problems. Eventually, the water-pump bearing burned out. That delayed us for many hours. A wheel came off our luggage trailer. Again several hours were lost. We were traveling through semi-arid country, where the temperature was 105 degrees or more during the heat of the day.

We do not exaggerate to state that it was wonderful to leave the heat of the plains behind. On the other hand, the reader can imagine the effort that was required to set up housekeeping in our hill station cottage. A cook and housekeeper must be hired, supplies for the kitchen purchased, clothing and bedding unpacked, and beds made up for six.

In short, everything necessary for living needed to be done. That didn't change the fact that it was almost too good to be true to have Gordon and Larry at home with us again."

"What a joy to see Breek's School and Lushington Hall where the boys live! Their dorm mother, Miss Reeve, is a wonderful woman and the boys think a great deal of her. The staff, too, is wonderful, and knowing this helps us when we miss the children so."

The boys went to school on weekdays. On sunny Saturdays when they were home from school, sometimes we all went to Ooty Lake, rented a boat and enjoyed rowing. After boating, an enjoyable picnic on a grassy bank of the lake completed our outing. That picture brings back many pleasant memories! Another delightful activity was strolling through the beautiful Government Gardens, just below where the boys lived.

School closed for two weeks, giving parents and children a little more time to enjoy each other. We filled those hours with as much enjoyment as possible, knowing that our time together was short. One of the favorite times of the day was family story hour in the evening. After a short devotional and a time of prayer, we read together the excellent stories that were appropriate for children of their age.

Even though time was short, tonsillectomies for the three older boys and Dad had to be crowded in. Everyone got along fine; and as a result of the surgery, Wesley's health showed marked improvement. Those precious times together were over much too soon. Before we knew it, we found ourselves preparing to send the boys back to boarding. The next thing for us was getting ready to return to Trimulgherry.

Just before we left, we learned that G.E. had major problems with his teeth and needed several removed to make way for his permanent ones. This, added to the sorrow of parting, was a difficult blow, and caused Lola to shed tears as we made our way down the hill.

A fifty-mile trip down steep hills and around hairpin bend after hairpin bend found us a little dizzy and somewhat nauseated at the foot of the Ghats (hills). This discomfort was magnified by the change from the cool at the top to sweltering heat at the bottom. Regardless, we pressed on to reach Bangalore–if we could.

Here let me mention that British India built what were called "dak bungalows" along all of the major roads. These were for the convenience of government officers on their tours of duty. In these dak bungalows was basic equipment for staying overnight (or several days, if needed. The bungalow usually consisted of a fairly large room that contained a table and chairs and a cot or two. Off this main room would be a bathroom with a flush toilet, in which there might be running water, or if not, there would be a large stone tank filled with water for flushing and for bathing. Outside the bungalow would be a caretaker's house. The caretaker usually did double duty as a cook. We tried to plan each day's trip to make sure we could arrive at one of these dak bungalows by evening. They were like an oasis in the desert–a very welcome sight for weary, dust-covered travelers.

In relation to this trip, I will mention only one other matter. Floyd and I agreed that he would tend to the car's mechanical problems and I would look after the tires. I wound up changing, patching and pumping up tires twelve times on that trip to and from the hills. Shoes from oxen, as mentioned earlier, were the major cause of all that work.

LANGUAGE STUDY

Language study was going to be the major ongoing challenge for the foreseeable future. We can't ever forget the hours and struggles we spent with language, and the feeling of triumph when notable progress was made. Other events that happened during those months stand out in memory.

We had hardly gotten resettled into life on the plains when a letter came from the school nurse saying that G.E. had come down with hepatitis. He just went through having several of his teeth pulled, and now this. Not to be with our children was always hard, but it was doubly hard at a time like this.

Just shortly after we received this news about G.E., Lola became ill. A mission meeting had been called at Bhongir. I came down with a severe migraine on that day and stayed at home with the boys so that Lola could go to the meeting. During the afternoon session, she began to run a fever and became seriously ill. The doctor diagnosed her with malaria and prescribed Atabrine. A day or two later, we noticed yellow color in her eyes along with other symptoms, and persuaded the doctor to take her off Atabrine and prescribe rest treatment for her hepatitis. Atabrine may cause severe liver damage, even without hepatitis, but when given for hepatitis could prove fatal. Lola did well with the rest treatment and, after a few weeks, was returning to health again. We praise the Lord for His guidance in this situation. While G.E. and Lola fought through their bouts with hepatitis, one by one Larry and Wesley came down with it. That made four out of six in our family attacked by this disease at one time. All did well, and before too long, were restored to health. Three cases of mental illness occurred on our compound at the same time. The wife of our Brahmin language teacher had an illness that affected her mind. After a few months, she passed away. The wife of one of our missionaries suffered mental illness which resulted in the couple being sent back home. A single, male missionary came down with cerebral malaria, causing him to be temporarily out of his mind. Thank the Lord he recovered in due time, but these experiences took their toll on our time, energy and emotional strength. During this time, Lola was involved in ministry to the young wife of our fellow missionary and I took time to minister to our teacher and his family.

In spite of the many distractions, Lola and I passed our first-year Telugu exams in early December. Jumping ahead a little–in our March 1953 letter, I wrote, "Lola and I have read in Telugu several chapters in the Gospel of John, and believe that the Lord is helping us make some progress in learning this difficult language."

Shortly after our exams, we had the joy of welcoming G.E. and Larry home from Ootacamund for nearly two months. To them and to us, it seemed like that time would never come. Lola says, "Meeting them at the station was like meeting family and loved ones in Heaven." She would describe their departure quite differently. Being growing boys, they enjoyed Mom's cooking and for the first few days, ate as if they had been starved.

A new family was put in charge of the station. The boys had new playmates to help keep them occupied and happy while we were busy with language study. Wesley and Verle were glad to have their older brothers home, but no doubt, the feelings were mixed since they had competition for Mom and Dad's attention.

The sky is always clear during India's winter, making it enjoyable to ramble about the neighborhood on the lovely, balmy evenings. Sometimes the full moon was as big as a bushel basket as it rose over the horizon. There were lots of new things to see and learn on these strolls. Some evenings another family walked with us, adding to the enjoyment.

Trimulgherry is a suburb of the twin cities of Secunderabad and Hyderabad. Our family custom for Christmas was to draw names and buy presents for the person whose name we drew. We rode the public buses and did shopping in the city. We visited both of the big cities, combining adventure and shopping. Among other pleasant outings were visits to the zoo and the park.

Some Sundays, we went into Hyderabad to attend a church pastored by K. Joshua. Occasionally, his family served a curry and rice meal that we learned to relish more and more. Other Sundays, we attended the Wesleyan Methodist Church just across the road from our apartment. This was where Lola taught Sunday school and, with the help of the boys, attracted so many children that the pastor of the church became alarmed. He remarked, "We can't have all of these Hindu children coming into our compound." The pastor's daughter helped Lola teach the class. Apparently, she did not hold her father's opinion.

In this way, the Christmas break quickly passed. All too soon, time came for G.E. and Larry to join other missionary children on their way back to boarding school. We drew heavily upon the Lord's help to get us through the sad partings that had now become a regular part of our lives.

That year (1953), during our stay in the hills, it became my turn to experience hepatitis. I came down with it shortly after our return to the plains. Because of our previous experience, we immediately recognized it and started the prescribed rest treatment. As soon as I felt well enough, we accepted an invitation from Fred and Cora Roth to visit them in their station at Mongol. We wrote about it in our October letter:

"Fred and Cora, who formerly studied with us at Trimulgherry, are working at Mongol. One weekend we went out to visit them and found ourselves in the midst of a cholera epidemic. Ten peopled died in the vicinity of their bungalow within four days. Roths did all they could to help the sick and no doubt saved several lives. Those who came for help and faithfully took the treatment recovered. At about three o'clock, a medical officer drove into the village and promptly disinfected every well with chlorine. Later he made plans to inoculate all who would come. We secured serum from him and gave each other shots. That was our first time to practice giving shots to someone else – an important skill on an isolated station."

We went to visit several of the stations during our two years of language study. To have exposure to many facets of the life and work in which we would soon be involved was valuable.

APPOINTED TO ADILABAD

Again we wrote in the October letter:

"Adilabad. This city is approximately two hundred miles north of Hyderabad City. The territory around is hilly – like low mountains – with forests and many wild animals, including leopards and tigers.

Before we moved to Adilabad, we faced exams for the second year of language study in late November. Both of us passed the orals, but Lola didn't quite make it in some areas

136

of the written examination. We could proceed, anyway, with our plans for moving to Adilabad."

In early December, the children came home from school, and we were reunited as a family for two months. That period each year was the time we all enjoyed more than any other. In late January of 1954, Wesley joined his older brothers on their way back to school. We faced an even more difficult parting, leaving Verle alone with us.

We began thinking about doing missionary work in India way back in 1944. Now after ten years, we had actually arrived on the station and were ready to begin our work. At the same time, we knew very well that we had much yet to learn. At least now we were on the field ready to begin the practical phase of that learning.

Some description of the physical setting will help to make our situation more real to the reader. Adilabad is a district headquarters, which is equivalent politically to a county seat in the U.S. At the time, the town had a government hospital as well as district government offices. Locally generated electricity was available in the city. Since our bungalow was outside the town, we were required to provide our own kerosene lighting and use our kerosene refrigerator.

There was no petrol pump (gas station) in town. The nearest source of supply for gasoline was at Nirmal, 30 miles south. We needed to be sure to fill the car's gasoline tank, and two auxiliary five-gallon gas cans that we carried with us, before we left Nirmal. In addition to auto, bus and lorry (truck) travel, Adilabad had a railway station and a railroad connecting us with the outside world.

Brother B.R. Opper built the bungalow and placed it in a spacious compound, surrounded by a mud and brick wall. The bungalow had a small kitchen, combination dining room and living room, two bedrooms and two bathrooms. A flat roof, just a foot or two above our heads, leaked in the rainy season. In the hot season, it caused the heat to be almost unbearable—with no electricity or fan.

We were blessed to have three servants: an old man named Krupia was our gardener, Lazarus was our cook, and a Christian woman named Ruth gave Lola help with the housekeeping. Krupia daily filled the large water containers in the bathrooms for the flush toilet and shower. Warm water for showers could be arranged by setting a bucket in the sun. In cooler weather, we used a charcoal water heater to heat water for bath and washing clothes.

Our washing machine, made in the USA, could be cranked by hand. Each tubful was usually cranked for fifteen minutes. Ruth helped with the weekly wash, as well as sweeping, dusting, picking stones out of rice, and many other household tasks. Lazarus lived with his wife and family in servants' quarters a short distance from the kitchen door. This made it easy for him to come to work, and convenient to call, if needed.

We soon came to know Yesudas (servant of Jesus) and Prakasham (shining one). Yesudas pastored a congregation in the palam (section of town) near us. Prakasham pastured a small congregation across on the northwest corner of town. I walked mile after mile to surrounding villages with Yesudas on my right and Prakasham on my left. In the beginning of our ministry together, my role was that of a companion and a student. These men were my teachers in this new culture.

Ideally, Lola should have had a trained Bible Woman to be her co-worker. In actual fact, the mission did not succeed in recruiting and training enough Bible Women to provide one as a coworker for each lady missionary. The mission reasoned that single lady missionaries needed such help more, because they did not have a husband and family to join them in the work. This posed a real disadvantage for Lola.

Working with my coworkers was a great help for me to learn the colloquial language. The local spoken language was very different from the standard written language we had studied. Lola worked with her servants and made steady progress in learning kitchen terminology, as well as common household words used by ladies in the home.

We had daily prayers with our servants and their families, and attended the worship service in Kanapur (the palam near us) on Sunday. In these ways, we were both getting more familiar with customs of the people and common vocabulary. After a few months, when the preachers spoke in public, we could understand quite well. The reason for this was that public speech was close to the more formal written Telugu. Another factor was that we steadily increased our Biblical vocabulary. (Village people always said that I spoke "book Telugu".)

We arrived in Adilabad in early February. The weather was warm and dry, the very best time for touring. Touring evangelism meant camping near one village for a few days, sharing the gospel in the best way we knew, and then going on to another village. We were eager to make as much use of this time as we could.

Jack and Ella Wilson, the missionaries we followed, came to live with us for a couple of weeks to help us get started. A few times, Lola and I, along with Verle, went with them in their '29 Model A Ford to villages where there were some Christians. Most of the time, just Jack and I went together and sometimes had short meetings in several different villages in one day. In this way, I became familiar with the field that was to become our responsibility. The Wilsons were preparing to go on furlough, and before long had to leave us.

To describe what we did after they left, let me quote from our March 1954 letter home:

"Our station was equipped with a crude, homemade house trailer for touring. We prepared it to be drawn by oxen, hired a team of oxen and a driver, and set out for the more distant villages of our field. Lola and Verle rode in the trailer and I followed on the cycle. Finding a good mango orchard near the village of Thosham, sixteen miles south of Adilabad, we parked the trailer in the trees and made camp for one week. Yesudas and Prakasham pitched a tent close by.

We created quite a sensation among the natives as we moved along, and then again when the people at Thosham learned that we were going to live near their village. Each evening we held meetings in the village, and in the mornings we went to smaller surrounding villages. Some of the forest people in these little villages had never seen a white family before and were visibly afraid. In spite of this, little groups gathered and patiently listened as we sought to show them the plan of salvation by means of singing, flannel-graph stories and preaching.

One night we held a meeting in Devapur, four miles from Thosham. The two preachers and I walked home through the forest at night. I carried a pressure lantern that gave off a brilliant light. Even so, every strange sound caused the preachers to start – for fear a tiger or leopard would jump from behind a bush. We arrived home safely."

I concluded that same March letter by requesting prayer that these tribal people might understand and receive the gospel.

(I should explain that mango trees put out fresh leaves and blossoms at this time of the year. Parking under a mango tree and in a mango orchard offered the best shade and the coolest place to camp. We also made sure there was a well close enough to give us a good water supply.)

In the above quotation from our March 1954 letter, I mentioned smaller villages in the area, and that people who lived in them were timid. Thosham is a Hindu community consisting of many different castes and some outcastes. The smaller villages are tribal. Tribals are animistic in belief and have chiefs and elders for their village government.

In that same letter is this article entitled "Ghonds":

"We are located in the midst of hill ranges and forests. Scattered through these forests is a hill tribe called Ghonds. These people are friendly. We think that many of them would respond to the gospel. As yet, no missionary has learned their language and, consequently, no solid work has been done amongst them. However, recently the Ghond language has been partially reduced to writing. This should make it much easier to learn it and use it. Pray that a way may be found to get the gospel to those people in their own language." (Our interest in tribals began at this time.)

HOT SEASON AND HILL SEASON – 1954

The month of April had arrived and the temperature in the shade was approaching 110 degrees Fahrenheit, making it blistering hot for touring. One could somehow endure the heat of the day, but sleep was very difficult at night. Though I might have lingered longer, Lola and Verle needed to go to the hills and get out of the heat. Both Lola and I needed to do more language study. It would be far more productive to do that in the cool, not to mention wanting to be near the boys. For that reason, the three of us packed up and went off to Ootacamund for the third time.

This time we traveled by railway to Trimulhgherry for our first stop. There we saw many of our friends, including the Wilsons. Jack and Ella were about to go to the hills too, where they would get their children from school and go on furlough. For that reason, the Wilson's were now ready to sell us their 1929 Model A Ford. Praise the Lord! The Bells had a car for the first time in India. Among the many advantages was it could pull the trailer, eliminating the need for oxen.

The trip from Trimulgherry to Ootacamund required three stages. An overnight trip brought us to Madras Central Station. From there we transferred across town from the Central Railway to the Southern Railway. Another overnight trip brought us to the station where we caught the hill train that would take us winding in, out, and around the bends, as we wended our way up to Ootacamund.

Only a few of these special trains in the world are engineered to climb up a mountainside. To do this, an extra rail with cogs is installed in the center between two regular rails. The engine is fitted with a cogwheel that meshes with the cogs on the center rail. With a combination of traction between the regular wheels and the tracks, plus the help of the cogwheel, the train moves slowly, but steadily, up the mountainside. Riding the hill train was a fun experience for all. The windows of the tourist-class passenger cars were wide open, permitting us to enjoy all of the sights, sounds, fresh air and delightful (or otherwise) aromas along the track. As the train wound its way slowly up the hill, we were pleased because the temperature gradually became cooler – a welcome relief from the steamy heat of the plains below. The appearance of trees and other vegetation visibly changed as we gained altitude. The fauna as well as the flora changed. Mountain birds and animals came into view. A new, refreshing fragrance came through the open windows. When the smell of eucalyptus mingled with the sight of eucalyptus forests on the mountainside, we knew that we were near our destination.

Breeks School planned for "sports day" to take place after parents arrived in the hills. G.E., Larry and Wesley were involved in races, high jump, broad jump and other sports activities. In addition to the excitement of having them with us again, we were eager to see them participate in these events.

We were also very keen to see how Wesley was doing in his classes, since he was just starting. Along with that, we were eager to assess the adjustment that G.E. and Larry were making to British school and culture – a factor very crucial to their happiness and learning capability. The first two years, they were both at the top of their classes. On this visit, for the first time, we began to see signs of some problems that in time became much more serious.

Six wonderful weeks for the family to be together were very soon over. In Lola's words, "Each parting was so hard." Before long, we were back at work in Adilabad.

"Youth for Christ is sponsoring a series of tent meetings to begin here on November seventh and conclude on December fifth. The tent is forty feet wide by sixty feet long and will seat, in Indian fashion, about four hundred people. After months of prayer and negotiation, we have secured a choice plot of ground in the center of town on which to pitch the tent. We praise the Lord for this victory. Now we ask you to join us in prayer that God will lead to the right speaker and interpreters. We work among Telugu and Marathi-speaking people and plan to have the message translated from English into both of those languages."

Later, in our December letter we wrote:

"Our YFC campaign is over, but the work is not finished. We believe that there will be fruit from the seeds sown for years to come. The attendance varied from 100 to 400, but there were many people who came regularly. At least 100 children learned the gospel story so well that they will never forget. There was Malliah, who put his trust in the Lord and gave a public testimony that thrilled our hearts. God answered prayer during these days, with the result of seventeen decisions. Continue to pray that these will grow in grace and the knowledge of the Lord."

In that same letter we wrote:

"A BIG STEP! Two years ago, our mission along with many other missions felt led to teach their people to stand on their own. Missionaries would likely be forced to leave India before long. The church must be ready for that day. Indian Christians need to be taught to trust the Lord and not the missionary. For this reason, we are asking the congregations on the Abilidad field to support their pastors. Preachers are being asked to do without mission support and trust the Lord to meet their needs – either through the help of the congregation or, as did the Apostle Paul, "by the work of their own hands." Our Adilabad preachers dislike this idea and oppose the plan."

Someone has said, "These were the best of times and the worst of times." That describes what it was like then. We had just concluded a fruitful campaign. We were having success in the literacy program. Out of that program, the brightest student, a Hindu young man, said that he believed in Christ and asked for baptism. He took baptism and was given the name Daniel.

At the same time, Yesudas and Prakasham, one on my left and one on my right as we walked to the surrounding villages, were filling my ear with their anger at being cut off from their salary. This was particularly difficult for a new missionary still struggling with a new language and culture. To add fuel to the fire, the mission sent two single lady missionaries to join the work in Adilabad. In order to make a place for them, the congregation in Adilabad was asked to vacate the mission building they had been using and go back to their own modest, mud-walled building.

The Christian community was upset and, in retaliation, they refused to say "Salaam" to us or treat us civilly (not speaking to us). Possibly the people knew we were not the authors of this action, but were simply carrying out mission directives. Whatever they knew did not change their behavior toward us. We felt the brunt of their anger and rejection personally.

This drove us to our knees in prayer. For us to rationalize this drastic move on the part of mission leaders was difficult. We were new missionaries struggling to master a new language and trying our best to understand the customs and thinking processes of a new culture. We would have dearly loved to have one of the older, more seasoned missionaries come and tactfully present the reasons for this radical change. No one came. We could only pray that the Lord would help us to love the people anyway, and keep our hearts right, by maintaining a right attitude both toward the mission and toward the people. I'm not sure that we were totally successful in this goal.

The policy permitted us to employ Yesudas as an evangelist. The offerings from the two congregations could then be used to support Prakasham. This alleviated the pressure on them somewhat and gave me a co-worker for village evangelism.

A DIFFERENT STRATEGY FOR VILLAGE
EVANGELISM

Field missionaries gave their reports in our annual meetings. One report especially impressed me. This missionary had visited 80 villages in a short span of time. I needed to evaluate the wisdom of that approach and ask the Lord what he would have me do. Putting together things I had read and my own reasoning, plus much prayer, I resolved that the Lord would have me do it differently.

From this time on, we planned to give enough time in each village to make the way of salvation understandable to people who had never heard. To accomplish this, we could camp in a village for ten days to two weeks – teaching simple songs that the children could memorize, telling the Bible stories with the aid of flannel graph, and emphasizing the simple basics: creation, fall, the birth of Jesus, some details about his life, the crucifixion and resurrection.

At the same time, we would visit with people individually during the day. By doing this, we hoped to gain rapport with them. Trust toward us would open the door for trust of the message we brought.

During these busy days and along with other challenges, family was always very major in our thinking. Letters to and from the boys in boarding were of special importance. Their health, academic concerns and happiness, along with their sense of well-being, were continually on our minds and in our prayers.

Now that Wesley was away at boarding, Verle had the privilege of enjoying Mom and Dad without sibling competition. That may have given him some special benefits. I remember having him sit on my lap as we read together. He made steady progress in his reading ability and was able to read quite well before he went to school.

Lola remembers some interesting incidents from that period in his life. The Ray Schrags lived thirty miles to the west of us in Kinwat. One day Ray came to Adilabad by train and walked to our bungalow. Verle saw him coming from a distance and excitedly came running to Mom shouting, "Mom, a Christian is coming! A Christian is coming!" He knew that we were Christian and that most of the Indian people around us were either Hindu or Moslem. Apparently another American symbolized another Christian to his young mind.

Verle was of special interest to the Indian boys and girls around us. On occasion, he gathered them around him and had a little preaching service all his own. Since he had been in

India most of his life, he was much more fluent in the Telugu language than his parents. No doubt Wesley, before he went to school, knew Telugu very well too. The three older ones had never lived on a mission station where the only language spoken, outside the home, was Telugu. At four or five years of age, we don't know just what Verle understood about the gospel or about what we were doing.

While we looked forward eagerly to his three older bothers coming home for Christmas vacation, probably Verle had mixed emotions. After they were home for a while, he asked, "Mommy, who do you and Daddy like the best?" He was facing an adjustment to the fact that he no longer had our exclusive attention. Then all too soon, he too was to go off to boarding school.

CHRISTMAS CELEBRATIONS

This year (1954) we were not facing language exams at the time the boys would come back from school. We made the 225-mile trip from Adilabad in our Model A and were at the train station in Hyderabad to meet them when they arrived on Thanksgiving Day. Friends invited us to celebrate Thanksgiving with them. Later, we took the boys to the

Quality Restaurant in Secunderabad, and for the first time, bought them Indian ice cream cones.

We stayed overnight in order to have a full day to make the trip back to Adilabad. That gave us time to exchange names and do a little Christmas shopping before we left the big city. This was the first time for the older boys to ride in the Model A. We had a very pleasant trip back to what was now our new home. G.E., Larry and Wesley had never seen Adilabad nor been in the bungalow. They seemed glad to have a house and compound to call home.

Balancing our duties as parents and our responsibility for and commitment to evangelism took a little doing. Yesudas and I almost daily walked to a village and proclaimed the gospel in whatever way we could, including distributing tracts and gospels. If we went and came back in the morning, I still had a good portion of the day with the family. On occasion, Yesudas, Prakasham and I went to another village in the evening.

We tried to plan some activities in ways that we could be together as family and carry on the work at the same time. The older boys could walk along with Yesudas and me on some days. Lola and I always planned at least one tour that included the whole family. This required packing cots, bedding, and supplies for six. Lola was good at organizing this and the boys helped.

One year we camped at Mavala, a few miles south of Adilabad. We found a good campsite with shade, water supply, and room for the tent and trailer. Some of the boys stayed in the tent with me. This not only gave us a chance to be together as a family, but also gave the people a chance to see us as real people. The boys fascinated the people. Because they especially loved boys, our sons helped open their hearts. Old grannies loved to pinch the boys' cheeks, just as they did their own children. I don't think our boys liked that very well, but they did not misbehave and offend these well-meaning elders.

When we returned to the bungalow, time had come to make some Christmas preparations. We looked around for something to use for a Christmas tree. Behind the servants' quarters stood a neem tree (margosa). It had many branches very close together. We cut one of the branches, built a wooden stand for it, and called it a Christmas tree. After Lola and the children finished decorating, it made a pretty Christmas tree.

The shops in Adilabad had just a few things that we could buy for presents, such as combs, soap and simple things. In addition, fruit would work for stocking stuffers. To say the least, the possibilities seemed quite limited.

One day I noticed a litter of puppies in a village. I talked with the owner who agreed to sell us one for the family. I took all of the boys with me and let them pick out a puppy. They soon agreed on one that they held in their arms, taking turns carrying him home. They named him Sport. No Christmas present we bought for them ever pleased them quite like Sport. When we fed him the cheapest whole grain in the market, he thrived and grew like a weed. Soon the boys were tearing around the outside of the house with Sport chasing them and having a great time. Lola's cooking did the most to make Christmas special. In addition to baking cake and pie, she made candy and roasted nuts.

The Hindus have many festivals. Some of them are very colorful and lavishly celebrated. For this reason, every effort is put forth by the Christians to make the celebration of Christmas very special. They buy inexpensive, colored powder and mix it with water to make watercolor. This they used to paint their mud walls and decorate their homes. Paper flags with various designs are fastened to strings to make streamers. These are criss-crossed in the church in such a way as to make it look festive.

The pastors and some of the men begin their celebration by starting caroling at midnight on Christmas Eve. They go from house to house singing carols until near sunrise. Missionaries and family must be prepared to be up most of the night, because different groups may come caroling at any hour of the night. This kind of night is followed by a Christmas worship service in the morning. This particular year, in order to mollify hurt feelings a little, we missionaries planned a Christmas feast at noon and invited all of the church people to come. (Usually we would leave this for them to plan.) In line with indigenous principles, we asked a small gift per meal. This was not to cover the cost, but following custom only. About 50 people came. In the afternoon, they gathered with their families to play games and distribute prizes, such as small bars of soap, combs and other useful items that were inexpensive. Our family joined in the afternoon program in various ways. The boys joined in some of the games. Lola and I took turns handing out prizes. We were considered dignitaries and were careful to do only those things they requested, in order not to offend in their culture.

Christmas festivities over, life settled down to the more routine. Our wonderful time to be together as a family passed all too quickly. Before we knew it, the boys had to go back to Breeks School.

Our March 1955 letter says:

"The past few weeks we have been living in the trailer and working in the villages. In several villages, we have had five-day campaigns. The first day we tell the story of creation, ending with major emphasis upon the creation of man and his fall into sin. We go from house to house in the morning, telling all who will listen. At night, the people gather around the bright light from our kerosene pressure lantern to hear the story and see the flannel graph pictures. We continue each day with a new story until the basic Gospel foundation is laid. The crowds grow from night to night wherever we have done this. Later we hope to go back to these same villages for five more days. As possible, perhaps two or three more times. Pray that the people will remember what they have heard, and that the Holy Spirit will use His Word to speak to their hearts."

THE MODEL A FORD

Any account of our first term in India would not be complete without some stories about our 1929 Model A Ford.

The wheels on the Model A were large enough in diameter to lift the body fairly high off the ground. This gave clearance for travel through deep ruts, over stony ground and occasionally over a low stump. Missionary work in those days tested every capability the equipment had.

I was anxious to get out to some of the more distant towns and villages as soon as possible, after the rainy season ended. The roads were dry enough after two or three weeks, but the streams kept flowing for quite some time after the rains stopped. We have colored slides showing us in the Model A trying to ford a stream and getting stuck. Another advantage of the Model A touring car was its light weight. Usually one could find a group of men working in the fields nearby. Just a few men could almost lift the car and carry it out of the mud. They could certainly push it to solid ground.

During our first Christmas season in Adilabad, we decided to go to Umri Hospital to get a checkup for the children before they went back to school. A trip from Adilabad to Umri required crossing the Penganga River. By this time, the rains had been over for three months and the river was low. We thought we could cross without any problem. We were wrong. The Model A made it to the center of the river and stopped. Several men came to help us. Very soon we were across and on our way. I don't remember any problem on the way back.

Annual Conference for the India Mission took place in late September. We made arrangements to meet Joe and Molly Jenkins in Nizamabad at noon on the day before the conference began. Nizamabad is a town about halfway between Adilabad and Secunderabad.

The day for the trip turned out to be rainy. Our open touring car had no curtains for the windows. The rain was coming from the west, which was on Lola's side of the car. She protected herself from the rain by holding an umbrella in the window.

Another detail to keep in mind was the windshield wiper. That Model A had a hand-operated wiper for the driver. Picture me driving in the rain, reaching up often to crank the windshield wiper, while Lola is holding an umbrella in the window to keep the rain from drenching her.

We arrived safely at the British Wesleyan Methodist Church compound on time. Joe and Molly Jenkins met us there. While we were eating our lunch, one of the lady missionaries came out to talk with us. She asked if she might ride with us to a town on our way. The Jenkins' car had windows; they could keep dry. For a reason I do not remember, they had no space for this lady.

We explained what it would be like in our car. She would have to use her umbrella to keep dry. She said that she could ride with her bishop, but that he was so near-sighted, it made her nervous to ride with him. She brought her bag, climbed in the back seat, and we were on our way again, with the Jenkins following closely behind us.

The rain became heavier as we drove south toward Secunderabad. I needed to crank the windshield wiper often. After an hour or two, we came to a "tank bund." In that part of India, the people constructed earthen dams that were called "bunds." These dams formed artificial lakes that were called "tanks," hence the term "tank bund." These artificial lakes provided water for irrigation of the rice paddies, located below them. The only way to pass through that area, either by oxcart or automobile, was to drive on the top of the dam. These dams were from an eighth to a quarter of a mile long.

I shifted gears to make it up the steep climb to the top of the dam. The process of shifting and steering up the embankment kept me from cranking the wiper. The windshield was so drenched with water that visibility was almost nil. Just as soon as I could, I cranked the wiper. Immediately in front of us was a herd of cattle. I hit the brakes very hard, but they were wet and did not hold very well. Somehow we managed to avoid crashing into any cows.

After some loud exclamations and catching of breath, we moved slowly through the herd of cattle and on to the south end of the dam. Now we faced descending from the embankment to the road below. That required shifting into low gear, paying close attention to driving, and braking to control the speed on the steep downhill decline. At the foot of the dam, I quickly cranked the wiper. To my horror, a bridge was washed out just in front of us. It seemed that there was no way to get stopped before we plunged into the roaring flood ahead. Suddenly, we smashed into a pile of gravel that jerked us to an abrupt halt.

Jenkins were so close behind us that they nearly smashed into our car. Joe jammed his car into reverse and put on the brakes. His quick thinking averted an accident.

Recovering from the shock, we surveyed the situation. How could we proceed? To the right of the washed-out bridge was a road under flowing water. We must measure the depth of the water to find out if it was safe to cross. After rolling up our pants legs and removing our shoes and socks, Joe and I carefully waded into the stream. It proved to be shallow enough for us to drive through. Jenkins had a rope in their car. By tying the rope to their bumper and ours, we could use the power of both cars to drag our Model A off the gravel pile.

After crossing the stream safely, we were soon at the point where our guest rider wanted to stop. With a twinkle in our eye, we asked, "Would you like to ride back with us?" She replied, "No thanks, I'll take the train." Some people just don't relish lots of adventure.

HIGHLIGHTS FROM OUR FIRST TERM

From our November 1955 letter:
"As I write to you, I sit in a tent which is pitched on the western shore of an artificial lake. The sun has just arisen above the forest which fringes to the opposite shore of the lake. My eyes are dazzled by the brilliant colors of red, orange and yellow that dance on the water before me. No, we are not on vacation. We have just risen to give ourselves a vigorous day of work.

You have guessed it – we are on tour. Our camp is about one-fourth mile from the jungle town of Mavala. They have heard the gospel from time to time, but as yet there are no declared believers. We feel led to camp here and work until some of the folks believe, and we can establish a congregation, or until they force us to leave. This is what we believe the Apostle Paul would have done. We trust God to bless us as we follow his example.

The people of Mavala are stirred up. Every time we walk into the village, we find the people talking about this 'new religion,' and these people who are insistently asking them to believe. Yesterday the village teacher called me to his house. At his house, we found the Hindu priest present with many of his disciples. They were determined to have a showdown on this matter. We presented the gospel message as clearly as we could, being careful to read clearly from the Bible as the basis of what we taught. We challenged the village priest to do likewise from his sacred books. He finally confessed that he knew nothing about salvation and that he was a sooth-sayer. Later that day, the priest threatened that anyone who dared to become a Christian would lose his employment. This is the power he holds over these people."

An article in our February 1956 letter states:"One day a lady came from the village with garlands and articles of food on a tray as an offering to the gods. She especially came to worship Lola. When we appeared in camp with four boys, she concluded that we were gods. Indian women feel blessed when they have sons and cursed when they do not. Lola had a Bible woman with her that day who could explain clearly that we were just humans like her, and that though we would not accept her gifts, we would pray to Jesus. He could answer her prayers."

Out of that Mavala effort, we could report only one man reading the Bible and showing interest.

Also in 1955, the lady missionaries reported that in the village of Ashapur (village of desire) four people prayed the penitent's prayer.

Our July 1956 letter reports:

"Rain quite largely restricts our activity for four months. What could we do to make that period fruitful? In answer to prayer, a good shop at a reasonable price and in a very good location became available. We turned the shop into a library. So far, we have had more young people interested in reading that we have books and space.

We have started a book club. For a small deposit, people are allowed to take books home to read. In addition, the children are offered a free Gospel of John if they memorize ten Bible verses. For memorizing fifty verses, they will receive a New Testament. In this way, we seek to plant the Word of God in their hearts. Pray that the Lord will lead us to an intelligent, committed Christian to operate the bookstore."

For an assessment of several months' work in the library, I quote from our November 1956 letter:

"We called it 'The Word of Life Library.' Its location was on one of the main streets of the city. With a wide front that opened onto the street, it was easy for many people who saw the bright books on display to drop in and look around. We sold some books, gave away many tracts and leaflets, and talked with many visitors who came daily to the library.

Among those who have been friendly, we ask you to pray for a Mohammedan man who has come to know the Bible and believes it is true. Pray also for a Hindu young man who has read several books and spent several hours with us in friendly conversation."

Our November 1956 letter also tells this story:

"HOSPITAL: For some time, we have known that Lola should consider another operation. After much thought and prayer, we decided that surgery should be done just after conference in the early part of October. The German lady doctor at Karimnagar Mission Hospital undertook the surgery on Tuesday, October 9 The ordeal is over now, and Lola is beginning to regain her strength."

In that same letter of November 7 we wrote:

"Excitement! Just two weeks from today, the boys are to start down the hill for home. Every letter shows their excitement. Of course, Mom and Dad are getting excited, too. One other item adds to our excitement. The older boys can't wait until we start back to America. This brings up a big question. WHERE SHALL WE LIVE?"

There was a school problem that loomed large at that time. All four of our sons were living in Lushington Hall and attending Breeks School. The boarding as well as the school were under British administration. We were glad that their philosophy was Christian.

However, more and more problems gradually unfolded during this time which were difficult, especially for the boys–and for that reason difficult for us as their parents. Both Gordon and Larry were praised for being at the top of their class when they started. Unfortunately, circumstances threw the two into the same class. The British way was to pit the two brothers against each other. They would taunt Gordon by saying, "If you don't get to work, your younger brother will beat you." This had the reverse effect of what they aimed for. By the end of our time there, in just three years, they had the two older boys failing in their classes. Another British practice that we seriously disagreed with was rating the students. We visited a class where Gordon and Larry were present. The teacher rated the students by pointing to them and stating, "These are at the top of the class and these are at the bottom of the class." This pedagogical practice was very repugnant to us.

When Wesley was in the third grade, his teacher informed us that he was failing in his classes. The primary problem was reading. During our time in the hills, his Mom and I spent quite a few hours helping Wesley with this problem. When he went back to school, he had improved so much that his nice young teacher confessed, "You have shown me that it was not Wesley's fault, but mine."

Apparently, a British notion was that having the older boys harass the younger ones helped the boys to grow up tough and ready to handle whatever came. There were other examples of physical abuse. At meals in boarding, a matron would slap the boys in the back of their heads if they weren't holding their fork, knife or spoon in proper British fashion. This happened unexpectedly in such a way as to make the boys afraid whenever an adult was anywhere near.

One of the Anglo-Indian teachers apparently had significant prejudice toward Americans. She said of one of our boys, "I knew he was a bad boy the first time I saw him." She had absolutely no grounds for this opinion, based totally upon prejudice. We approached the principal for his advice. His response was, "The other children are doing well. Your boys don't have what it takes." These words were discouraging to us, to say the least.

In fairness, it needs to be pointed out that the school had some new problems of its own. Under a new policy, they had recently opened their doors to Indian boys and girls. Most of them had a weak background in English and other subjects. In order to help this new group of students, the teachers were forced to give much of their time and energy to bring them up to speed. For that reason, they had little time to give to the other students.

A second element enters into this problem. The British had a practice of hiring tutors to help their children outside of class and during vacations. We did not learn of this until later, and could not have afforded it anyway. Being as generous as we possibly could, for the sake of our sons, we felt that either we could not return to India or must make other arrangements for their education.

Among the adjustments missionary children have to make is the time when school opens and closes. American schools open in September. The Breeks school year began in June; summer break took place beginning mid-April. For that reason, we arranged to ship our heavy luggage to Bombay ahead of us, and then went to Ootacamund in mid-April to see the boys finish their last weeks of school and take part in sports activities. Then we made our way to Bombay to meet our ship and embark on our homeward journey back to the United States.

Explanation of our school problem may give the impression that we went on furlough to solve that problem. The problem was big enough to warrant it, but actually our five year first term was up and it was time for us to go on leave.

We planned for enough time in Bombay to be sure that all final items were taken care of to ensure that we did not miss our ship. This done, we had a free day or two to see the sights in Bombay. Among those sights were the beautiful Hanging Gardens. We have lovely slides to bring back memories of the fun we had together in the gardens. Some of the boys wondered if Bombay was America.

This paragraph is from our July 1957 letter:

"Our voyage was by way of the Cape of Good Hope. The long journey gave us thirty-two days at sea. We enjoyed the extra ice cream passed out in the morning and afternoon. Twice when we crossed the equator, the officers on board held special ceremonies. Neptune was introduced in these programs, and the children were told to watch for the bump when we crossed the equator."

OUR FIRST FURLOUGH

On the return voyage home, our first stop was at Cape Town. One of the memorable events in Cape Town was a cable car ride to the top of Cable Mountain, while Mom– because she couldn't stand heights–watched from below. When the boys leaned over the cable car railing and called, "Hi!", Mom couldn't look. The boys had their first escalator rides in Cape Town.

The next stop was at the Canary Islands. We were impressed with their beauty, but surprised that, even though it was a frequent stop for passenger ships, practically no one spoke English. We found ourselves trapped in a shop during noon curfew. The proprietor told us that we couldn't leave and stood near the door with a banana knife in her hand. One of the ladies in our group gave her a push to the side. We marched safely out, though a bit shaken.

Visiting England was a very different experience this time. We stayed at a more pleasant guesthouse for missionaries, instead of the House of Rest. Spring was in the air, and we enjoyed riding on the top deck of double-decker buses to see the great city. Westminster Abbey was interesting. Among other things, we saw the changing of the guard at Buckingham Palace. A kind and generous British lady gave Lola a warm, woolen, suit to wear. She also gave the boys some money. Most of the time that we were seeing historical sights, they were restless to go and spend their money.

Lola and I enjoyed seeing the children react to things that were new to them. Watching the numbers jump up and down in the window of a cash register fascinated them. One of them was trying to find out how the heat got into a department store, when there was no visible stove or furnace. Some of them puzzled for a while to figure out what to do with the thumb, when trying to put on gloves. These old, familiar items to us were forgotten or completely new to them.

Someone from the Mission Office in New Jersey met us at the pier in New York. They helped us arrange for the shipment of our goods to Detroit and put us on the train for the Jersey City office. We stayed overnight at headquarters. The next day, our dear friends the Cranston Bernstorf's came and took us to their home in Philadelphia. Cranston was professor of anatomy at Hanumon Medical College in Philadelphia. We enjoyed a brief visit in their home.

Dick and Laura Witherell pleasantly surprised us by meeting us in Philadelphia and taking us to their home in Detroit. After a brief visit in their home, we made contact with Lola's mother, her sister and family, as well as my brother Leonard and family. No one had room in their house for a family of six. We needed to find housing as soon as possible.

The first item of business was to find a car. Rev. Chalmers Boring, who helped us after the fire, took me to the car dealer who had recently sold him a car. A salesman showed us a 1951 Nash Ambassador Super. He said to me, "Take the car, try it out, show it to family members, and come back in a few hours." I did that, and after thought and prayer, we decided to put out a fleece. If the dealer would sell the car to us for $150, we would feel that it was right to buy it. When I drove the car back to the lot, the salesman was near the gate and signaled to me. I rolled down the window to hear hi m say, "The manager has decided to let you have that car for $75." That settled it. We bought the car.

After buying the car, we found that it was using a quart of oil every 30 miles. Considering what we paid for it, that was not very surprising. We added oil often and did necessary traveling that way for some time.

The next thing to face was finding a place for our family to live for one year. Soon after we arrived back in the U.S., we attended the funeral of Lola's Uncle Rianzi. His wife Katie had died a few months earlier. With both of them gone, their large farmhouse was vacant. We hesitated to approach Lola's cousin Elon right away about renting the empty house. We decided to look a little longer and see what might work out. After another week or two of bouncing from pillar to post, we got up courage to ask Elon if he would consider us as renters. He was delighted when we asked. Our moving in would give him time to make plans for disposal of this parents' home. We would be helping him, and he helping us.

Lola had been praying for a home in town. I had been praying for a country home. God demonstrated that he could answer such conflicting prayers. He gave us a farmhouse in the city limits. The large house provided plenty of room for our family. In addition, there was a roomy garage, a big barn, a lovely garden plot, as well as apple and pear trees. Neighbors kept two ponies in the barn and let the boys ride them. We purchased two calves for them to raise: Shield and Pinky. This house was close enough so that the boys could walk to school. Truly an amazing provision for us. I know that we were thankful at the time, but probably couldn't fully appreciate what a wonderful provision it was. To God be the glory!

An auto parts store and machine shop were not far away. They agreed to help me overhaul the car. Our roomy garage gave me an excellent place to do the job. I tore the engine apart and found only one badly-scored cylinder. A mechanic from the machine shop rebored that cylinder and took measurements for rings, a new piston and bearings. For another $75, I was able to purchase repairs. By doing the work myself, the purchase price and repairs combined cost us only $150. Almost unbelievable! For that amount we had a car that ran beautifully for thirty thousand miles. After it was overhauled, the engine did not use oil and got more than 20 miles to the gallon. This car was our first to have an automatic shift, and drove and rode like a limousine. Praise the Lord!

We were settled in our fabulous home. The car was ready to go in just the nick of time. Assignments started coming that were to take me east, west, north, and south. What a great privilege it was to meet many kindly, generous people of God.

When feasible, especially while the boys had summer vacation, we went as a family. Among the most notable events of that summer was a trip to Seattle. We put our luggage in a carrier on top of the car. Three of the boys rode in back and one between us in front. The round trip was close to 5,000 miles. Outgoing, we traveled south of Lake Michigan and Chicago, going west. Returning, we took the northern route via Northern Michigan and crossing the Mackinac Bridge.

A family reunion was planned while we were in Seattle. This gave the boys the opportunity to spend some time with Grandma and Grandpa Bell and their uncles, aunts and cousins on my side of the family. We have some pictures to refresh our memories of this event.

Back at home, September was upon us with school was about to start. The garden was bursting with produce and the trees were laden with fruit. Careful planning was required to get everything done between my various meetings.

Lola had family members who attended the United Brethren Church in Hillsdale. We attended there some and found the people friendly. The church met our need in many ways. Unfortunately, obvious tension existed between the pastor and his people. Following a difficult first term in India, we felt the need of a healing atmosphere during our furlough.

After visiting several other churches, we eventually went to an evening service at Hillsdale Free Methodist Church. Following the service, the pastor invited us to the parsonage to get acquainted. That began a wonderful friendship with Dean and Ione Parrott. Our long association with the Free Methodist Denomination began at this time too. Hillsdale Free Methodist Church had an excellent program for children and young people. The pastors friendly invitation helped to confirm our decision.

After attending the church for several months, the pastor invited us to join the church. We had withdrawn from the United Methodist Church before we went to India. That our family have a church home was important to us. After thought and prayer, toward the end of our furlough, we accepted Pastor Parrott's invitation to join the Hillsdale Church.

Our October 1957 letter stated:

"It seems clearly evident that Lola will once again have to undergo surgery. (This will be the third time she undergoes an attempt to repair damages caused from childbirth.) Correction of her trouble is necessary before we can consider going back to India. Dr. Brown of Zion, Illinois, one of our supporters, gave us encouragement to believe that successful surgery could be done. That wasn't all he did. He paid the hospital costs. In addition, his wife Miriam took Lola into their home for the recovery period. What a fabulous gift to us! We shall be eternally grateful."

After several days, Lola recovered enough to return home. In the meantime, Grandma Kelly had been with us at the farm and helped run the household while Lola was away. Grandma was with us most of that year. What a blessing to have her help while Lola continued to recover from the surgery.

All four of our sons fit right in at their various schools in America. Their work came up to standard and from this time onward, none of the boys had significant problems with their studies. All are college graduates and have done well in their chosen occupations or professions.

Not long after school started, Larry's teacher called Lola in for consultation. The teacher explained that every time she came near Larry, he would duck his head or dodge to the other side of his desk. When Lola explained what had happened at Breeks School, the teacher was appalled.

One day the boys were playing football in the yard. Wesley enjoyed that kind of rough and tumble, and played hard. While playing, he tackled an older boy. Wesley hit his head against a belt buckle, hurting his head. Wesley said nothing about the incident for a few days. By the time he came to us complaining about a sore on his head, a serious infection had developed in his scalp. A large carbuncle formed. Gradually, all of the hair in the infected area had to be removed. When the spot finally healed there was a bald spot approximately two inches in diameter.

The doctor felt that it was wise to keep Wesley out of school because of the way the public reacted to a sore on the head. He feared that public treatment of Wesley could create psychological problems. For that reason, he was set back for one year in school.

AT THE CROSSROADS

In our October 1957 letter we wrote:

"Pray that if it is God's will for us to return to the field, He will make clear to us the ministry He has for us and any preparation we need to make for it now."

In spite of the many extremely negative experiences and challenges of our first term, I felt that the Lord had not released me from His call to India. However, no way would we consider putting the boys back in Breeks. For that reason, we began correspondence to make application for change of schools. Kodaikanal School in the Palni Hills of South India accepted our application. We found a place for them at Clancullen Boarding, also.

After finding a solution to the school problem, we began our preparations for five more years on the field. Our letter of June 1958 has this comment:

"GOING FORTH. Once again we are made to rejoice that the 'One Who Sends' has promised to go before. We are purchasing, packing and planning these days to the tune of 'Anywhere With Jesus.'"

One item that had to be planned for was the auction sale of the farm. Although furlough time is just for a year, many things have to be acquired for housekeeping. Before going back to the field, those things had to be disposed of. Lola's cousin Elon had sold us the furniture left by his parents in the old farmhouse. We had acquired an old car for Lola's use when I was away on deputation. (After a dear friend helped us paint it, it looked pretty good and brought a pretty good price at the sale.) The boys had bikes and two calves that were getting big by now. Actually, the calves were an attraction to some of our neighbors who knew that they would be pets. This would make them easy for their children to show at the fair.

The boys were disappointed when the auctioneer pretty much gave the bicycles away. The disappointment about the bikes was made up for in part because the calves sold surprisingly well. The sale turned out very well. The proceeds helped us to buy the remaining items needed for another term in India.

When the sale was over, our wonderful year in the farmhouse was ended. Lola's cousin Elon and his wife Helen put us up for the night. The next day we piled into the Nash Ambassador Super and took off for mission headquarters in New Jersey–our last trip in that wonderful car. Leaving the car at headquarters for them to sell, we shipped out a second time to the land of India.

Finally in the July 1958 letter we wrote:

"PRAY: for strength and courage for all of us as we part from loved ones again."

FINAL YEARS IN THE INDIA MISSION: 1958-1960

Our next newsletter was sent from Peddapalli, Andra Pradesh. It tells the story so well, I wish to copy it here.

"Dear Friends: Praise God for His protecting care that has brought us safely to our present home in India! This voyage had its new adventures and items of interest about which you may enjoy reading.

We had two happy days in England with Christian friends, and enjoyed fellowship with two different congregations on Sunday. There was a tense hour on Tuesday morning when we arrived at Tilbury and found that our reservations had been cancelled. After an hour of working on the matter, accommodations were restored. We went on board with a prayer of thanksgiving.

At the outset of this trip, G.E. was rather proud that he was to be treated like a man, because he required a full-fare ticket. His brothers rather envied him at first, but before long

G.E. was wishing that he were younger and could join in with the games and parties for the children.

The Strathnaver altered her course to stop at Marseilles, France. This gave us opportunity to visit the historic city, and to set our feet on French soil. Later that day, the ship drew near to the Island of Stromboli, where we saw an active volcano for the first time. You can imagine the fun as the boys, with cameras, took turns sitting on Dad's shoulders to get above the crowd for picture-taking. A small eruption was visible while we passed. The rumble of the explosions could be plainly heard on board ship.

For the first time, we traveled on a one-class ship. The boys had great fun exploring the whole ship. There were sports of many kinds, and most of all they enjoyed the large swimming pool–especially on the steaming hot days through the Red Sea. These activities, together with studies, made the days pass quickly.

The night after we left Stromboli Island, an Anglican priest left suicide notes, and then quietly stepped overboard. In the course of our voyage, there were four deaths. Our four news-gatherers brought varying reports. We often had to seek some official source to be sure of the story. At any rate, the two older boys had the news straight enough that they witnessed two burials at sea.

Customs delayed us for four days at Bombay, because of the parcels we had brought for others. One parcel had so much duty levied on it that it was not worth the price to bring it through. We succeeded in getting it released to send back to America. Fortunately for us, all of our own things came through, but duties were high.

Much work needs to be done on the Peddapalli Field. Pray that we may be used of God to strengthen the pastors and congregations. The boys will be with us until January. Meanwhile, we are trying to keep their studies progressing.

Sincerely in Christ – Gordon, Lola and boys"

The next letter states:

"The boys are finding plenty to do. They help Mom with the dishes, make their beds, and go shopping for us. Mornings are usually taken up with their studies, while Mom is kept busy with supervising. Around four p.m. they often go to play with the boys at the mission school not far away. Now that they have a longer time on the plains, they are learning a lot of Telugu.

Just now there is an added attraction. A circus has set up in the field next to our bungalow, about a stone's throw away. The music begins at 8:30 in the evening and goes on until after midnight."

That letter refreshes my memory concerning my involvement in several things. While on furlough, I contacted an owner of a peanut butter factory. I told him of my vision to help Indian people economically and hopefully add protein to their diet. He helped me acquire two hand-driven peanut butter grinders. These I brought to India with me. I was busy constructing a building and inventing the equipment needed to establish a factory. I found an old oven and installed a drum to revolve inside the oven for roasting the peanuts. I also devised a machine for rubbing the brown husks from the peanuts, to get them ready for the grinder.

We had some modest success with the project, producing more than one thousand pounds of peanut butter. The rainy season hindered evangelistic touring and gave time for the peanut butter project. By late September or early October, we were able to get back to the work that was closest to our hearts.

Touring on the Peddapalli field took us, first of all, to the villages where there were small congregations and self-supporting preachers. Our concern was to be able to encourage the preachers and their congregations. In our February letter, we reported that in three different villages backsliders confessed sin and set matters right. In the last village, named Elvaka, we had a special thrill when six young people responded to the invitation to accept Christ.

During the Christmas holiday, we took time out to celebrate Christmas as a family. We also joined with the Peddapalli congregation in their celebrations. These very special days for our family pass all too quickly. In January, we faced sending the boys away to boarding school again.

In our February 1959 letter we noted:

From Kodaikanal, the boys wrote, "It is just like America." Obviously, they liked their new situation. Their home away from home was called Clancullen. For fun and competition, the home was divided into three clans. Our boys were trying to help their clan win by learning memory verses. Along with their academic studies, G.E. was taking trumpet lessons and the other boys, piano.

In the meantime, word had been coming from time to time that the congregation in Adilabad was building a new church building. In our August 1959 letter we wrote this:

"Those of you who have been praying for the Adilabad congregation will be glad to learn that the church building has been completed. There has been a much improved spirit

185

of late. Pray for the Rusts and their ministry there. Rusts have started a bookstore ministry in the same place where we had ours."

A MOVE TO CLANCULLEN

Wayne and Evelyn Saunders were in charge of The Evangelical Alliance Mission (TEAM) boarding home, called Clancullen. When the time for them to go on furlough our very close friends the Chamberlins suggested that we consider taking charge of Clancullen while the Saunders were on furlough. When the Saunders requested us to take their place from January to October 1960, we were ready to accept their offer.

An automobile was needed to carry on the work at Clancullen. We had no car at that time and none was offered to us. Hindsight tells us that we should have made provision of decent transportation a condition of our acceptance. We didn't do that, and paid very dearly in wasted time and headaches because of it. Saunders invited us to spend the last two weeks of the 1959 school year with them. It provided an intensive exposure to the care of forty missionary children. A mumps epidemic broke out which infected nearly every child. We became involved in the care of the children, along with learning about purchasing supplies, accounting, managing the kitchen, and all the other matters related to daily routine. Because of the mumps, having the children ready to go home in time to meet their travel schedules added to all of the other stress.

The Lord blessed us; the children recovered, and their travel home worked out.

We saw the Saunders off on furlough. Then we made our way back to Peddapalli. We needed to be back in Kodaikanal in just a few weeks, ready to receive the children in boarding.

That short period involved a flurry of activity, including purchasing an old wreck of a car and trying to make it useful for the work that lay ahead of us. We were so busy that memories of that Christmas vacation are very few. One special memory does stand out. Lola and the boys were having a hard time thinking of something to give me for Christmas. They got an idea while discussing this with Bill and Joyce Scott, fellow missionaries at Peddapalli. We needed an auxiliary gas can to carry with us in our travels. Scotts sold them an old one. The boys painted it with a fresh coat of green paint. That was my special gift on Christmas morning.

Belongings had to be packed and shipped either to Kodaikanal or for storage in Trimulgherry. Peddapalli bungalow had to be left empty for the next occupant. We needed to get back to Clancullen a little early, to make sure everything was ready for an influx of forty children at the boarding.

After a couple of days at Mission Headquarters in Secunderabad, the six of us piled into our station wagon and started on our trip to the hills. About fifty miles out, I noticed a group of people walking along the side of the road. In India, it was wise to sound the horn and give warning that we were coming. I sounded the horn, yet the people continued walking along the side of the road. This gave every indication that they knew we were coming, and that it was safe to drive past them. Suddenly, some of the people veered onto the road. I braked hard to slow down and the same time swerved to miss the people. A new brake system had been installed and tested, but when put to such a severe test as this, the brakes threw us sideways. The combination of things caused the old station wagon to roll over completely on its top. We were slowed down enough to give us the sensation of an elephant gently rolling over on its back.

Driving in the sun had been warm. Everyone, except G.E. and I, were asleep. What a shock to find one's self upside down in an overturned car. The first questions that came to me were, "Am I alive? If I am alive, how much am I hurt?" G.E. immediately began to call, "Turn off the ignition." Fortunately he had recently read about the danger of fire in such cases. I turned off the ignition promptly and was able to climb out of the wreck almost immediately. G.E. was next, and soon everyone, but Lola, was out. We helped her out and set up one of the folding cots for her to lie down. She had a gash on her forehead just below her hairline.

Very soon the older boys were heard saying, "We prayed for a safe journey before we started out this morning. Now see what has happened." Admittedly that thought must have come to most of us. On the license plate were the letters APY. Lola looked at them upside down and remarked, "They don't look very APY now."

The body of the station wagon was crudely built from wood. When the wagon rolled over, the doorposts on the side of the impact, broke like matchsticks. Six of us were in the car, and except for Larry's badly scratched up arm, and Lola's scalp wound, all of us came out without even significant bruises. The next question we asked was, "How in the world did we come out of this so safely?"

We looked around to see what had saved our lives. To our amazement, the auxiliary gas can, my Christmas present, jumped between the top of the front seat and the roof. All the weight of the chassis was resting on that sturdy gasoline container. At the last minute, when we were packing, we had shoved that can just behind the front seat. It might seem like a mere coincidence to some, but to us it was the definite hand of the Lord. How marvelous is his watchcare. PTL!

Some positive memories relate to that scene. A government bus came along almost immediately. The driver stopped the bus, men got off the bus and joined together to set our station wagon upright. The driver of the bus took Lola and the children on board and transported them to a clinic in the nearest town. The doctor at the clinic stitched up Lola's scalp and gave Larry first aid. A lady missionary, a good friend of ours who was stationed in that town, came to visit Lola and the children at the clinic.

I stayed at the scene until the police wrote up their report. By propping up the roof on the broken side, I was able to get in the driver's seat and drive the old wreck to the town close by. Then all of us were invited by our missionary friend to spend the night in her bungalow. These were unbelievable provisions for our needs. Leaving the wreck behind, we caught the bus back to Secunderabad.

Ray Schrag, our friend who formerly lived in a station near us when we were in Adilabad, was now in Secunderabad. He graciously helped me get the old wreck into the city and promised to see what could be done about salvaging it. (In time, Ray had the wrecked body removed and a pickup body put in its place, but that vehicle never proved useful to us. We were glad when someone wanted to buy it and took it off our hands.)

In the meantime we made arrangements to travel by train to Kodaikanal. Fortunately our original plans allowed for enough extra time. We were able to get settled in boarding and have things ready when children began to arrive.

LOLA'S MEMORIES OF CLANCULLEN

"I could not have done the job alone. Two housekeepers (ayahs) helped with cleaning, doing the washing and ironing, making the beds for some of the smallest children and any other housekeeping chores. Two cooks and a butler helped prepare and serve the food. The cooks knew their job and were a wonderful help. I suggested menus for each meal and took note of supplies needed, such as meat, bread, milk, fruit, vegetables, flour, butter, peanut butter, jams, jellies, and syrup.

"Breakfast time was daily checkup time. Saunders had a merit system in place. The children received points for good hygiene. If they brushed their teeth, cleaned their nails, and properly did all the things required for a week, they received a star.

"At noon Gordon and I took lunches down to school. Our vehicle was an old truck, which the children affectionately called the Ark. We opened the endgate of the Ark and from there distributed the food to forty boys and girls. Just think of having an endgate party nearly every day. The gymnasium was just across from our usual place for lunch. The roof of the gymnasium extended a few feet beyond the front wall. On rainy days the children could gather there and stay out of the rain during their meal.

"Afternoons gave a little breather before school was out in the evening—time to take a little rest, read something, have a quiet time or catch up on details. Soon enough it was time to welcome forty children back for teatime.

"We planned to make the evening meal more substantial and satisfying for everyone. When their tummies were full, the children could handle homesickness and loneliness better at nightime. After supper I had devotions for the smaller children in our bedroom. Time for devotions was a time to let them gather around and get to feel close to me. After devotions came time to play, before they went to bed.

"Time for bed was also the time they missed their mommies and daddies most. The smaller ones wanted me to hear their prayers, give them a hug, a kiss and tuck them in. I loved to do this and soon became attached to each of the children. However, I was usually tired and ready for bed when the time came."

GORDON'S ROLE AT CLANCULLEN

The current word to describe my job at Clancullen is gopher. Whatever was needed, it was my job to "go fer it." Wood was required for the fireplace and the cook stoves. I purchased all of the supplies Lola needed for the kitchen, laundry and running the household. Chopping the wood into useable size for stoves and fireplace was a daily chore. Migraines were effectively worked out on the woodpile.

Clancullen was more than a mile up a steep, winding road from the school. Soon after breakfast I took a load of children down the hill in the Ark. Two trips were required in the morning and again to bring them home in the afternoon. At noon Lola and I took the childrens' lunches to them. Shopping for groceries and supplies was usually coordinated with one of the trips – most often after the second trip in the morning.

Kodai kids nicknamed the bazaar, where fresh meats, fresh vegetables, and groceries could be bought, the "Budj." A limited amount of fruit was usually available, such as bananas, oranges, papaya and jackfruit. The choices improved when certain fruits were in season, such as apples, pears, apricots, plums and mangoes. First quality beef was available at the meat market. (I mention quality of beef, because only very poor quality beef could be bought on the plains.) We could buy chicken, mutton and fish. Muslim merchants handle those meats, but have nothing to do with pork. From time to time pork could be purchased from Catholic farmers on the hill. Several grocery stores, operated by Muslim merchants, supplied other items such as rice, wheat, macaroni, and spices. Canned goods (the British term is tinned) were available on a limited basis and were quite expensive–jams, jellies, syrup, cheese, peas, corn, green beans–to mention a few.

We were very pleased that we could buy everything needed to prepare good, western-style meals. We don't remember that grumbling about the food was very prevalent. Some children were used to more sweets and dainties than we were inclined to serve. Although we had everything needed to prepare western meals, missionary versions of curry and rice were very popular. We probably had some variety of curry and rice, as a main meal, three to four times each week.

My favorite time of the day was after supper. The teenagers would gather in the front room for devotions. What an opportunity as well as challenge to have a little Bible study and prayer time with these young people. Often two or three of the girls would linger after devotions were over. This gave opportunity for getting more closely acquainted and on occasion to share burdens, inner struggles or problems.

My opportunity with the boys came at other times and in different ways. I visited with them in the boys' dorm. We went on hikes together, or I played ping-pong with them. They said their memory verses to me. What a potentially fine group of young men they were. Most of them went on to make a responsible contribution to their generation. Ours was only a tiny part in their lives along the way.

AN EVENT THAT WOULD CHANGE OUR LIVES

Let us back up a little to the time we were at Peddapalli. I went to Yavatmal to attend the annual Holiness Association Meetings being held there in October. At that time I met Dr. Frank and Mrs. Betty Kline, Rev. Roland and Mrs. Muriel Davis, Rev. Floyd and Mrs. Edna Puffer. We had met Dr. Paul and Mrs. Jessie Yardy earlier at their home in Umri. When the missionaries learned that we had joined the Free Methodist Church during our furlough, they began to urge us to consider changing missions.

Now that we were in charge of Clancullen, the Klines and Yardies had children with us. The parents learned more about us through their children. When their parents came for hill season, they had opportunity to get to know us better. In the course of events, Dr. Kline conferred with Dr. Lamson (general mission secretary), and was authorized to officially invite us to join the Free Methodist Mission. Some weeks later, after the missionaries returned to the plains, they sent Rev. V. B. Samudre and Mr. R. N. Gavankar, two outstanding members of the India Free Methodist Church, to interview us. That was in August or September of 1960. We clearly remember entertaining them in the living room at Clancullen. These men took back a favorable report. As a result of this we planned to go directly to Yavatmal from Kodaikanal, rather than returning to Secunderabad.

This decision was made in September of 1960. We finished out the school year at Clancullen. In late October, the children went off to their homes on the plains. Staying on in Kodai for a few days, we caught up on details, and tried to have everything in good order for the Saunders, when they would return in early January of 1961.

The boys were ours to enjoy again, without competition. That was special for them and for us. One of the things we did at this time was take a trip over the "forty-mile round." (This is the name the young people gave to forty miles of road they traveled with their bicycles. This road goes in a circular fashion starting and ending in Kodaikanal.) On the way we stopped at Lake Berijum. An old wooden boat, which the boys could make to float, provided a favorite sport for them. They paddled around in that for a while. Lake Berijum was at a lower altitude and a little warmer—very pleasant for our picnic lunch. Soon we traveled on to complete the forty-mile round, enjoying the beautiful sights along the way.

It was not easy to leave the India Mission. Some of our dearest friendships were made during the language study years. While there were some serious frustrations with mission policy, leaving our friends was a sad event in our lives. At the same time we looked forward to new challenges and new opportunities in an all-new situation. With mixed emotions we made plans to leave Kodaikanal and travel to Yavatmal. A new chapter of our lives and our journey in India was about to begin.

The weather in Kodaikanal had become wet, blustery and disagreeable. What a relief to return to the plains in late October in time to enjoy the most delightful season of the year. Our train tickets were purchased for the destination of Wardha, the nearest station to Free Methodist Mission Headquarters in Yavatmal.

The six of us were met at Wardha and taken to Yavatmal. There we were entertained in the home of Frank and Betty Kline. The Klines occupied the principal's bungalow on the campus of Union Biblical Seminary. So much happened in such a short time that those first days are just a blur in our memory. In a day or two, Dr. Kline took us from Yavatmal to Wun and helped us settle in our new home. At this point it is sufficient to say that our bungalow was spacious and more attractive than any of our other homes so far in India. We were delighted, especially for the sake of the boys.

EARLY YEARS AT WUN

The time from late October until early January was largely occupied with getting to know our new friends and co-workers. Rev. John Ramteke was pastor of the local congregation. We attended services regularly, though they were in the Marathi language that we didn't understand.

A Telugu speaking pastor, Rev. David Mamidiwar (Pastor David) was shepherd of a congregation in Rajur. Rajur is a colliery (coal mine) town, five miles west of Wun. Workers in the coal mine were largely Telugu-speaking people. Employers preferred to hire Telugu workers because they were more willing to do this work than the local Marathi people.

Pastor David was not as well educated as Marathi workers in the conference; nevertheless, he was energetic and loved his people. They responded to his love and filled his little church every Sunday morning. The church building was too small, for one thing, and had just a dirt floor for another. Pastor David was eager to improve the building. He persuaded a local merchant to supply him with cement for laying a concrete floor. The boys and I used our Jeep and trailer to help haul sand and gravel to mix with the cement. We worked hard with our shovels to fill the trailer and then unload it near the church – giving us a practical way to identify with the people of that congregation.

Sometimes on Sunday we attended the Telugu services at Rajur. We enjoyed being able to understand the message and entering into the song service. On occasion I preached in Telugu while Pastor David translated into Hindi for some in the congregation. In this way a warm fellowship began between us, Pastor David, his wife and his family. He was to be my co-worker in village evangelistic tours for several years to come.

OUR FIRST CHRISTMAS INMAHARASHTRA

The city of Nagpur replaced Secunderabad as the shopping center for food supplies and other goods. Getting to Nagpur from Wun was quite an undertaking. The shortest route was more than one hundred miles over some rough roads.

We planned this to be our Christmas shopping trip, a family occasion and as much fun as possible. We needed to get an early start. For that reason preparations began the day before. Lunch was prepared and stored in the refrigerator. We planned to explore on the way, and then to shop for food supplies and take care of any other business required. A return trip of over two hundred miles was itself time-consuming. Even with an early start our return home would be late.

Each of us had a family member to shop for. Items that American children would dream of for Christmas were not available. Using our imaginations and donning a spirit of adventure we did the best we could to enjoy it. There were details that tried to run competition with our enjoyment.

In Central India, December weather is relatively cool. Even so, any sunny day is warm. Except when we could park in the shade, the Jeep was sweltering hot. Swarms of people were everywhere. Because we were a white family, we never ceased to be objects of curiosity to them. In spite of some of these difficulties, we managed to get our shopping done and find some interesting things to see and do. In this way we succeeded in taking with us some pleasant memories.

The Hindu Festival of Lights occurs a few days ahead of Christmas. The bright lights and fun activities associated with the festival made it tempting for Christian converts to revert to and participate in non-Christian practices so familiar in their past. Christian leaders wisely planned alternative activities for these days. Pastors encouraged their people to attend what they called "Family Week Services." In preparation for "Family Week," Christians gave their homes a fresh, bright, color wash and prepared decorations in a way similar to that we described at Adilabad. Each evening during that week, the people gathered for a service. Since Christmas came just a few days later, their decorations and other preparations worked for both occasions.

We planned to have our family Christmas on another day so that we could give our energy to joining with Indian Christians in their celebrations. We prepared to receive carol-singing groups throughout the night on Christmas Eve. On Christmas morning we attended their worship service and in the afternoon our family took part in their games.

It is also important to highlight the fact that our family times were very, very valuable to us. All too soon our brief times together were over and the boys returned to school in Kodaikanal.

TOURING IN THE VILLAGES

Our India Chimes of February 1961, tells the story. "We are working in a new territory. There are no Telugu congregations in this area. Telugu villages are scattered along the north bank of the Penganga River. These are just across the river from villages we worked in before.

"Free Methodist missionaries and Christian workers were Marathi-speaking and for that reason had not concentrated in this Telugu-speaking area. In the course of events, we found ourselves in places where the people had not seen white people before.

"Two good tours were carried out in January. Pastor David, from the Rajur Church near Wun, came along as evangelist on these tours. We conducted meetings for eight nights in Mukutban (moo-koot-bun.) Then we moved on to the village of Patan (paw-tun), spending seven days there. Each day we visited surrounding villages, preaching in a total of twelve different villages.

"In the village of Patan a young man of the Reddi caste showed keen interest. (The Reddi caste was often the highest caste in the village. They were the landowners and the people with power and prestige.) We will tell you more about him in our next letter."

Then, in our India Chimes of April 1961, we wrote:

"In our last letter we promised to tell you the story of Deva Rao, a young man in Patan who showed much interest. Deva Rao was just a small boy when his parents died, leaving him an orphan. His father's brother took him and reared him as his own son. Deva Rao grew into a fine stalwart man. His uncle learned to love him as he loved his own children.

"Because of his honesty and sincerity, Deva Rao is highly respected in Patan village and holds a seat on the town council. When we came to Patan, Deva Rao had plans to go to Adilabad on business. He attended our meetings on the first night and decided to postpone his trip to Adilabad for one week. He not only attended all of the meetings, but also came to our camp several times to learn more. One day one of his friends came with him and wanted to talk about America. Deva Rao said, "No! We want to learn more about what the Bible teaches."

More about Deva Rao later.

Another story from that April 1961, letter: "In the Telugu hamlet on the far west side of Wun, about twelve people were ready to take baptism a few years ago. A Hindu young man, seeing their interest, threatened to report this to officials. Because of fear, all of them held back.

"Some three months later, that young man became sick and died. This filled all of the community with fear, believing this was an act of God. Last night that entire hamlet, from grandpas and grandmas down to babes in arms, came to listen to the gospel for more than an hour. They still wanted to hear more and invited Gordon to come again."

That April letter contained this personal note, "Lola left on April 3 to join the boys in the hills. Annual conference will be over on April 25 and Gordon will join the family about May 1."

After Lola left for the hills, I attended a Free Methodist Annual Conference for the first time. The conference took place on the campus of Union Biblical Seminary. Missionary personnel were as follows: Roland and Muriel Davis, Frank and Betty Kline, Paul and Jessie Yardy, Mel and Betty Pastorious and Gordon and Lola Bell. Normally conference takes place in early March. By the month of April the weather is much too hot for foreign guests, such as a Bishop or the General Secretary of the mission board. The conference was late that year which is the reason that Lola and Jessie Yardy went to the hills before conference.

I think that Bishop Taylor presided that year. Conference business was primarily about the older established work. I kept eyes and ears open to learn all I could. Pastors and national officers of the conference gave their reports in Marathi. I understood very little of what was being said. The bishop had an interpreter by his side. Probably someone interpreted some for me as well. Other than a report about the Telugu work, my part in the conference was very minimal.

The sweltering hot weather added to my eagerness to be on my way to the hills to join Lola and the boys. For the first time we were to live in Free Methodist housing. Missionaries had purchased what was called Blackburn property. Included in that estate were Blackburn Bungalow where the Yardy family lived, the Kline Bungalow, Blackburn Cottage where the Davises lived, and Blackburn Orchard Cottage where the Bells were to live.

Blackburn Orchard Cottage was nicknamed the haunted house. The dilapidated property required a lot of work to make it liveable for our family. The three older boys slept in a room downstairs that was dark and damp. On the main floor, we rigged up a partition of sorts that created a small bedroom for Verle and a larger one for us. Our bedroom was over a breezeway. The cracks in the floor let us look through to the out-of-doors. Strips of coir matting (cheap matting woven from coconut fiber) helped to improve that situation and protected our feet from the cold floor.

A small kitchen and dining room helped to make our living more pleasant. A fairly decent living room with a fireplace made for a cozy family setting at night. We had devotions together followed by family story time. Then there was time for study, mending or just enjoyable reading.

Except for two weeks of vacation, the boys went to school five days out of each week. Kodaikanal School planned the school program to fit the schedules of American parents. One of the events we looked forward to was Sports Day. The boys all participated. Lola and I enjoyed watching events and were proud when one of ours won a prize.

Mr. DeYong was the music teacher, giving both private and group instruction.

G. E. took lessons on the trumpet and Wesley on the clarinet. Mr. DeYong considered his music as a ministry. We were thankful for his godly influence on our sons.

We enjoyed the students' music recitals. Another night of entertainment included numbers from the school orchestra. The highlight of school activity was the school drama. Some years the productions were truly outstanding. Always they were some-thing to look forward to, especially for people who had neither radio nor television throughout the year.

Graduation exercises took place at the end of the school year. They were planned to take place near the middle of May. Most parents were up from the plains by that time. Most missionary parents attended graduation exercises. If our own children were not involved, children of our friends were. This brought the school year to an end and gave the children two weeks of vacation before the new academic year started. For families due for furlough, graduation was the signal to begin the journey back to the homeland.

VACATION TIME IN KODAIKANAL

To clarify the picture, note the ages of the children at this time. G.E. would be 16 in August and Larry would be 15. Wesley was 13 and Verle was 12. Their ages determined the type of activities we planned together. Kodai Lake was a favorite place for an outing. At the boathouse we rented one punt and one rowboat. Having three persons per boat was about right. Mom sat in the bow of the rowboat while two others rowed. Sometimes she enjoyed taking her turn rowing. The lake was sufficiently large that rowing around it from end to end a time or two, gave us all the exercise and sightseeing we desired. Somewhere along the way, we enjoyed a picnic lunch, bringing the boats side by side near shore.

One of our choice places for a hike was Bear Shola which was about a half hour's walk from Orchard Cottage.

Part of the attraction was a little waterfall with a pool at its base. Scrambling up the side of the falls, we could make our way to a level, grassy place to lay things out for a picnic. The boys could climb to their hearts' content, throw pebbles into the pool, look for animal and plant life in the water, or whatever. Mom enjoyed being with her family and watching them have fun.

OUR ANNUAL TREK TO ELEPHANT VALLEY

One of the important summer events at this time in our lives was a trek down the mountain to Elephant Valley. On the first day out we descended four thousand feet. At that level the temperature was warm, and keeping comfortable overnight was not difficult. On these treks we saw wild elephants, sometimes a tiger off in the distance, and occasionally herds of bison.

Quite early in the evening, we searched out a place to spend the night. We usually chose a cave. Next, we gathered plenty of wood for a fire, not only to prepare our meal, but also to maintain a bonfire through the night. Leopards, tigers, bears and other wild animals would be less likely to come near because of the fire. We felt safe that way and took turns keeping watch while others slept.

On these excursions we were not interested n hunting or disturbing the life of wild creatures. We were more interested in watching them from a distance and taking pictures. After two nights camping out and climbing four thousand feet back up the mountain, we had our fill of adventure. Sore muscles added to the relief of arriving at home. It was great to take some rest and enjoy the comforts of more civilized living. Soon the time came for the boys to return to boarding and for Lola and me to go back to our work in Wun.

OCTOBER TOURS

Pastor David's brother-in-law and wife had been contacted to come and work with us. Not only could Yesudas help me as a co-worker, but his wife Pushpamma had Bible training and could help Lola with her work among the women.

Another development at this time was a visit from Mr. & Mrs. Jeevanandam. They were studying at Yavatmal Seminary and sensing a call to rural evangelism. They were to take part in two tours later in the year. Below is the story as told in our November 1961 Chimes of India.

"Mr. & Mrs. Jeevanandam joined Lola and me on two tours in October. We camped six days in Bori. I remind the reader that a hotel keeper had shown keen interest back in February. This gentleman, named Datatre, was even more interested this time. A wealthy farmer provided a new site for our meetings by opening the gate to his court-yard so that people inside and out could hear the messages. This man attended the meetings every night. On the last day he came to our tent confessing his wicked life. Much of his wealth had been gained by wicked practices. He asked, "Is it possible for your Jesus to forgive a man like me?" What joy for Mr. Jeevanandam to explain to him that Jesus came "to seek and to save that which was lost" (Lk. 19:10) and that Jesus said, "Him that cometh to me I will in no wise cast out." (John 6:37).

THE BOYS COME HOME FOR CHRISTMAS

In the Chimes of February 1962, "Our house was invaded by a gang of young fellows the other day and there hasn't been a dull moment since. Of course we look forward to this invasion, but it is always a bit of an adjustment after being childless for several months.

"Samuel the cook left us early in December and G. E. volunteered to take his place. He was a good help to Mom in the kitchen and kept at his job until after the big event on Christmas day.

"The boys joined us on an eight-day tour to Mukutban. Our Land Rover has an electric fuel pump, which is supposed to end fuel pump problems in hot weather. This one gets lazy every time it gets warm. We learned that tapping the pump with a screwdriver would keep it running. Gordon and Larry took turns sitting on the fender and with the hood up they could keep tapping the pump. Mom worried while Dad drove carefully. We arrived a little late, but safely, at camp. We later learned to wrap the pump with a rag and keep it wet.

"Before our family tour to Mukutban, a man from that village came to visit us at Wun. We were away at the time and Pastor David shared the gospel with him. At the time he seemed to be broken, confessed his sins and accepted Christ. During our tour he attended meetings regularly and invited us to hold meetings in his home. One thing brings doubt about his sincerity. He keeps asking us for a loan."

I went back to the mission station in Wun to carry on the work there. The times of long separation from the children were hard enough, when Lola and I were together, but to have her absent along with them made it doubly difficult. We remember these sacrifices as the truly difficult part of our missionary career.

THE MUD HOUSE IN SUNNA

In the Chimes of October 1962, we wrote, "We felt led for some time to try to get closer to the people. By living in tents we managed this in the dry season, but there was no way to do this during the rains. We used some of our project funds and repaired a fallen-down building in the village of Sunna that had formerly been used for a church. Walls around for privacy and a roof overhead to protect from the rain provided the basics. A mud floor was bearable once it was plastered with cow dung to keep the dust down."

While Lola was away in the hills of South India, this seemed to be an ideal time for me to try a new experiment. By reducing my equipment to the lowest minimum for my survival, to the best of my ability I would try to identify with the villagers on their economic level. One morning after the men had gone to the fields to work, the ladies came to see how the "sahib" carried on his housekeeping. During their visit I overheard this remark: "What in the world does one man need with all of these luxuries?"

I had the final answer to my question. Nothing I could do would bring me closer to their economic level. I must ask the Lord to help the message to resonate with them despite the difference in our cultures.

I was very happy when the time came for Lola to return home. Now we could talk things over and face things together. The problem of school for the boys loomed large in the near future. In a letter to Hillsdale Free Methodist Church, dated January 4, 1963, are these words:

"Gordon and Larry will likely return to the U.S. next May. We are considering Central College High School for them in McPherson, Kansas."

In that same February letter we wrote about the other missionaries and their families joining us for Christmas: "It is quite a task to prepare a special meal for twenty-two people in India, but we had a good time together at the table and during the afternoon. Presents were exchanged and each Free Methodist missionary family contributed to the program and meal."

Since we were quite isolated at Wun, having a houseful of these delightful people was doubly exciting — truly, the distinguishing event of the 1961 Christmas season. Pleasant memories still linger.

THE YEAR 1962

During the month of January, after the boys went back to school, we held a two-week series of meetings in the village of Sunna. We also made return visits to Mukutban and Patan.

Earlier I wrote about Deva Rao. In the Chimes of February 1962, we wrote, "Deva Rao's attitude has changed. Last week when we were in Patan, Deva Rao obviously avoided us. When Gordon managed to corner him, he was politely friendly, but quickly found an excuse to walk away. We do not believe that this is a personal feeling against us, but rather the result of threats and intimidations, which came after his expressed interest.

"The same has been true of Sombayya, whom we mentioned in our Christmas letter. In fact it has taken place on the part of the majority of people who have expressed interest. Let us not give up, but keep on praying.

"Day after tomorrow we shall return to Patan for two weeks. We hope to see Deva Rao again. He was busy with election activities last time. Perhaps he will have more time on this visit."

The summer of 1962 brought a crisis to our family. Circumstances arose that made it necessary for us to take our children out of Clancullen Boarding. The result was that we had to make arrangements for our sons somewhere else. Finally it was decided that Lola should stay with the boys at Blackburn Orchard Cottage and three boys from the Turner family would join them. Lola became dorm mother for seven boys.

These concerns were in the back of our minds as we carried out tours after the rains came to an end. The children returned home in late October. We were together again and that alleviated some of the anxiety momentarily.

In the Chimes of February 1963, we wrote, "From October 22 to November 4 a team from Yavatmal Seminary assisted us in conducting evangelistic meetings in the coal mining town of Shasti. From the first there was open opposition to our meetings by a self-styled prophet who rented his own public address system and conducted his own meetings after ours were over. As far as we could tell, this simply stirred up interest, drew larger crowds and made our meetings more effective. Quite a few Christians live in that community. Without leadership they are somewhat backslidden and in spiritual defeat. The result of our ten days there was a new desire on their part to be organized and build a church. They have started a building fund with the hope of building soon. We praise the Lord for this."

Again from the same letter, "While the boys were home, we took them with us to live in the mud house at Sunna for one week. This was one more step in getting acquainted. The people are showing more friendliness, but more openness is still needed. Some weeks later, just before the boys went back to school, we took them to Patan. The people were so pleased because our whole family came to see them. One of the ladies insisted that we come to her house. Then she called her neighbors and said, "See, our relatives have come.""

The following paragraph from the above letter gives an interesting glimpse into our lives at that time. "We returned from camp at Soona on Saturday. Mom had been wondering all the way home what to plan for lunch. Camp supplies were depleted and there were no supplies at home. She dreaded the groans if lunch had to wait until after shopping before cooking could happen. Imagine her delight when we arrived home and found that the first food parcel from Hillsdale Free Methodist Church had arrived. A couple of soup packets helped to save the day."

A VISIT TO AGRA AND THE TAJ MAHAL

We did not fully know how our family crisis was going to be solved, but it was quite certain that G.E. and Larry would not be coming back to Wun—and for that matter, perhaps not to India again. For that reason we planned a trip to New Delhi and Agra.

Our friends, Cranston and Eileen Bernstorf, with their children, came down from Pakistan to join us on this excursion. Many historical sights kept us busy trying to take them all in. Old Delhi was the capitol of the Mogul empire. These Moslems were famous for their outstanding architecture. In Old Delhi the Red Fort and Kutub Minar were among other fascinating sights.

In New Delhi we saw the beautiful United States Embassy building. The boys thought it was the best. The highlight of our trip was seeing the Taj Mahal, truly the most magnificent sight of all. We spent several hours looking at this awe-inspiring building from different angles and in the changing light. We took away from this trip memories for a lifetime.

The boys returned to school in early January. We planned to make another visit to Shasti because there had been so much interest shown there. Unfortunately, for the second time, I came down with hepatitis and had to lie low for weeks.

In the meantime, the mission decided that we should return to America to work out the educational problems for our two older boys. This meant that Lola had to take the heavy load of packing and making arrangements for closing out life in Wun and getting ready to travel. The Womens Missionary Organization made arrangements for us to live for a few months on the campus of Seattle Pacific College. For that reason we planned to go to Kodaikanal, take the boys with us from there and travel to Colombo, Ceylon. We would board ship in Colombo and take the eastern route this time.

A book could be written on the whole trip from Wun to Kodaikanal, to Colombo and to Vancouver, British Columbia. The Sorbo family traveled with us on the journey from Kodaikanal to Colombo. In Colombo we embarked on a French passenger ship. It stopped at Singapore and Saigon as well as at Hong Kong on the way to Japan.

At Hong Kong the Alton Goulds drove us by car to a point where we could look across the border into China. They also escorted us on a tour of some of our Free Methodist housetop schools. At night it was our privilege to attend an evangelistic meeting in Hong Kong. We enjoyed the Goulds and very much appreciated the special glimpse they gave us into our Free Methodist work there.

Next stop was Osaka, Japan. The Lavern Sniders enthusiastically introduced us to the ministry of Osaka Christian College. They also took time from their very, very busy schedule to show us some of the churches in the Osaka area. A cherished experience was the chance to sit on straw mats and visit with a Japanese Christian family in their home.

Traveling by train from Osaka to Tokyo, we were graciously received by the Bill Huletts. He had secured accommodations for us in Tokyo, and he and his family helped to make our visit in Japan very special. Their teenage daughter took the boys on a tour of Tokyo. No doubt that was a treat both ways. However, the boys missed the wonderful reception we had at Immanuel Bible College. We visited the school and were the invited guests to a sukiyaki dinner at the home of Dr. Tsutada, the principal. This visit was especially fortunate since we met Joshua Tsutada there. Joshua and other young people from Immanuel Bible College eventually came to Union Biblical Seminary. Some of them became our close friends.

From Tokyo we embarked on a British ship named the Orosova. We enjoyed the British cuisine better than the French and were more at home with the activities on board. The Orosova's first stop was Honolulu. We had a full day for sightseeing on the island. Among the first things to impress us were the huge American taxis, compared to the mini-cars familiar in India and Japan. Perhaps the most impressive sight was Punchbowl National Cemetery. It was awesome and sobering to see long row after long row of crosses and think of the lives lost in that great war. This cemetery represented only a portion of the bloodshed and loss of life in that war.

Native dances, demonstrations of Hawaiian food preparation and a visit to a department store or two, among other things, made up our day. We were frankly eager to get on to America and to see our loved ones.

On the final leg of our journey, there were rumours of a sailor being murdered by his comrades. Sailors carrying a casket were the first people to disembark when we landed at the port in Vancouver, British Columbia. It was clear evidence that indeed, at the very least, someone died.

To our surprise and delight, the pastor of Vancouver Free Methodist Church, his wife and some members of his congregation gave us a royal Canadian welcome at the dock. They gave us a tour of Vancouver, including a view of the city at night from a mountaintop overlooking the city. To make it even more special, they treated us to a grand meal at a Chinese restaurant.

After spending the night on the ship, we had our luggage trans-shipped to a passenger train bound for Seattle. The six of us secured seats together in a compartment and traveled to the border, where we were met by a U.S. custom official. We had just finished our morning devotions. Six Bibles were on top of the first bag the official asked us to open. When he saw them he said, "You're O.K. You don't need to open any more bags."

This was the first and only time we came from India and landed on the West Coast. It meant a lot to me that my Dad and Mom were at the Edmonds station to welcome us. After a good meal at my parent's house, they took us to Seattle Pacific College and helped us get settled in our temporary home on campus.

A FEW MONTHS IN SEATTLE

Seattle First Church became our temporary church home. Mendel Miller was our Sunday school teacher and Bob Fine was our pastor. Floyd and Edna Puffer had retired and were living on Etruria Street, just above the college. They did much to make our stay on the campus enjoyable. Edna, in a way, adopted Verle, had him help in odd jobs and paid him a little for his effort. The Puffers had us over for wonderful curry and rice meals several times. Floyd contacted Bub Pound to help us get the used car we would need for our furlough travel. Bub came up with a clean, 1955 Chevy wagon in good condition that served us well for that furlough.

My mother and father, as well as several of my siblings including my eldest brother Oscar and his wife Katie, my third brother Warren and his wife Elaine, and my sister and her husband Vern were all in Seattle. William, second oldest brother and his wife Lenoma lived in North Bend, Oregon.

On one occasion William and Lenoma came up from Oregon for a family reunion.

On many weekends some of the family got together either at our house or at one of their homes. Croquette was a favorite outdoor activity, partly because many of us could join in the game. Dad loved to play horseshoes. Several of us joined him in playing that game. Many times we just sat around and talked.

THE BREAK-UP OF OUR FAMILY

In our letter of March, 1964, we wrote, "Wesley and Verle must fly back to India in order to get there as soon as possible after June1. They have prospects of traveling with another family, leaving New York on June 5. Gordon and Larry will be moving to their homes for the summer while Mom and Dad will take in part of the General Conference and follow to India a little later in June."

The Southwestern Company of Nashville, Tennessee, had summer sales opportunities for college students. G. E. made plans to join a group of college students from Greenville College, working for this company. He had some rough jolts to start with. Later he wrote to us from Corpus Christi, Texas,

"I have been experiencing something new and wonderful the last few days. I have met the Lord in a new way. I often feel His presence, and it is just as if He is knocking on those doors with me." (There is no way to put in words the joy this letter brought to us.) G.E. had good enough book sales that he saved enough money to go to Seattle Pacific that fall.

In our letter of July 1964, we wrote, "Mr. & Mrs. Martin Kilgore of Hillsdale, Michigan have a new boy in their family. We are most thankful to them for providing a wonderful home for Larry and a chance to finish his high school in Hillsdale next year.

"Lola is enjoying taking an active part in local church activities, including her work as superintendent of the junior department in Sunday school. In addition she has had several calls to show slides in this area. Hillsdale has become hometown to our family, and both pastor and congregation have done so much to make life rich for us.

In deputation so far, Gordon has traveled over eleven thousand miles and has taken part in more than seventy mission meetings. His travels have taken him from Victoria, B.C. to Miami, Florida, and from St. Catherines, Ontario, to Caldwell, Kansas. To meet old friends again and make many new ones has been great."

Fast forward to November 1964, when Chimes says, "Faces of friends from Hillsdale Church, waving goodbye at Metropolitan Airport in Detroit, linger in our memories. It was especially hard to say goodbye to Larry, who stood with others, watching us take flight."

"The only exciting thing about the trip was the take-off," Verle wrote in his first letter from India.

"With earth so far beneath us, we had very little consciousness of motion. In fact the whole flight seemed like a dream. Our dream was rudely interrupted when we stepped off the plane in Bombay Airport on July 8th. The hot, humid air of that monsoon morning was such a contrast to the air-conditioned atmosphere on the plane that we felt like we were entering a Turkish steam bath. Committee meetings, account books, correspondence, legalities and technicalities — all this was waiting for Gordon. He was in an executive meeting the next morning after landing at Nagpur at midnight."

1965 HILL SEASON

In late April, we traveled by Jeep more than 1,000 miles to Kodaikanal. When we arrived, fog and dampness lay heavily upon the hilltop. We should have felt depressed because of weariness from travel and the lateness of the hour, but Wesley and Verle came running at the sound of our horn. All feeling of gloom was instantly dispelled. Wes and Verle had the cottage all ready for us and with pleasure we started another hill season in Kodai.

While in the hills we wrote a newsletter. Here are some quotations from that letter: "Wesley earns a little pin money making sure that piano students keep up their practice, while Verle adds to his spending money by helping the librarian. Wesley will soon be an eleventh grader. Verle, our little boy (six feet), will be in the tenth grade.

"G.E. made out quite well in his first year at Seattle Pacific College. Larry has had a good year with the Kilgores in Hillsdale, Michigan. Larry will join G.E. this summer in selling books for the Southwestern Company. Their selling will take them to strange places and require a lot of travel. They need your prayers these days. Pray that they will earn enough to attend Seattle Pacific College this fall."

TRANSITION FROM EVANGELISM TO ADMINISTRATION

Rather quickly, the responsibilities that the mission placed upon me made it more and more difficult to find time to be involved in evangelism.

In the above Chimes we wrote, "Clackity, clack goes the typewriter and rattle, rattle goes the brain. Early and late has not been enough to keep up with the volume of work. Stacks of work came along to the hills. In addition, there are new responsibilities here in Kodaikanal, such as school board meetings, religious service committee meetings and property matters."

A pleasant time with Wes and Verle passed all too quickly. A working vacation made the time seem all the shorter. Before we knew it, we were back on the plains continuing our work there.

Davises and Klines had already left the field. Yardys left for America from Kodaikanal this summer. Dr. Yardy had prepared Gordon to understand the business affairs of the hospital. Lola and I were soon to be the only Free Methodist missionaries remaining in India. Among my duties were: chairman of Umri Hospital board, involvement in conference affairs, sitting on Union Biblical Seminary's governing board, and participating in the administrative affairs of Kodaikanal School. All of these responsibilities might not have been overwhelming to some men. They certainly were to me.

THE BELLS MOVE TO UMRI HOSPITAL

Chimes, of January, 1966. "Dr. Bell! That is what Gordon is called around this place at times. At least we try to help the doctors. Why?

The Yardy family completed their commitment to India and returned to U.S.A.

Dr. Lysander, groomed to take Dr. Yardy's place, received a scholarship and financial help to attend Columbia University.

Dr. & Mrs. Fidler just completed their first year of language study. The ways of India are still very new to them. It is too soon for us to ask them to take over all of the responsibility of the hospital without help. We are trying to give help with the administration.

Muriel Davis, a trained accountant, formerly did the treasurer's work. The mission accounts included a journal to receive all of the daily entries. Each of those entries must be re-entered, according to category, in a ledger, of which there were twenty-three. The combined total amount of all the ledgers must equal, exactly, the total in the journal. For example, a separate account would be kept for the bungalow maintenance, another for travel, and still another for car upkeep. For a trained accountant, successfully handling these accounts would be no problem. For a novice, like Gordon, it was a terrific problem.

People came in with their problems all day long. In order to make any headway with the accounting Gordon had to work very late at night. Accounts have to balance to the penny. Often a slight copying error or a mistake in addition took hours to find. A special adjustments account gave the biggest headache. Sometimes the home board sent amounts that were first put into this account and then dispersed to other accounts. Sometimes the treasurer was requested to deduct amounts from some account and refund the mission. Keeping track of the ins and outs of that special account required understanding and precision.

With no training in accounting, this responsibility was a formidable challenge to Gordon. Many days the strain was so great that he suffered a severe migraine as a result.

Fortunately his health held until he learned how to do the job. After that the struggle was greatly reduced.

With that background, the reader will better appreciate this paragraph from Chimes, January 1966. "Half of each day is taken with hospital administration; the other half with mission treasurer's work. The latter is not so difficult since we understand it better. It does take time though, and combining the two jobs pretty much uses up all of our time and energy."

From time to time Gordon was invited to preach at Umri Church. In November 1965 he was invited to have a six-day series of meetings — a special opportunity as well as a great challenge. God blessed with several seeking salvation on Sunday morning.

Our moves to Umri brought us closer to Telugu-speaking people. From time to time we reached out from the hospital to keep in touch with villages in which we had ministered before, such as Sunna, Patan and Pandharkawda. Weekends gave opportunity to have meetings in the local villages.

The government of India started building a large dam across a river near Umri Hospital. Telugu workers were recruited for this project, since they were known to be willing to work much harder than the local people. We found about ninety of these Telugu people. They were living in temporary housing in order to be close to their work. Many of these people seemed to know the gospel and loved to sing the Telugu Gospel songs. Because they needed encouragement to live according to the light they had we took opportunity to minister to them, inviting to either accept Christ or to draw closer to Him.

Obviously the building of this dam was important to Umri Hospital as well as to the larger community. A dam creating a large water reservoir, would benefit thousands of people in this area and provide irrigation for thousands of acres of land. A second crop during the dry season would not only increase income for farmers, but also increase the agricultural output significantly. Another benefit would come from stocking the reservoir with fish. Because Indian people suffer for lack of protein in their diet, tons of fish will help to solve that problem locally. Yet another benefit would be raising the water table in the area. Umri hospital always suffers from water shortage before the rains begin. This should help solve that problem.

VACATION TIME FOR WESLEY AND VERLE

The two boys came home in late October. Living on Umri Hospital campus was a new experience for them. Both of them loved the Lord and were ready to pitch in and do what they could. Umri Hospital had suffered from serious embezzlement problems for years. One of the weak spots was the dispensary. In Chimes, January 1966, we wrote, "Wes and Verle have been counting pills by the thousands. They come home for meals smelling like medics. This is a big job, but we hope that a better inventory on the medications will help to prevent so much theft from this department."

For a few days, we managed a family tour to Sunna. Wesley befriended a high school youth by the name of Vital. Vital came from a tribal background, did well in Sunna public school and went on to high school in Pandharkawda, a village just five miles south of Umri Hospital. Vital often attended Gospel meetings being held regularly in Pandharkawda by teams from Umri Hospital.

THE VIJAY SIDAM STORY

To better understand what happened in Vital's life, one needs to know his background. Many years ago, Rev. and

Mrs. Root, together with their Indian co-worker Rev. Govind Kinker, camped near Sunna for village evangelism. At night they took their bright lanterns to a central place in the village and told the Gospel story to the people. In the daytime Rev. Root and Rev. Kinker visited from house to house. One day they found a mother deeply concerned for the baby in her arms. Rev. Root put his hand on the baby's forehead and found that the tiny girl was burning with fever. Upon Rev. Root's suggestion, Rev. Kinker laid his hands on the little one and prayed in Jesus' name that God would heal her. The Lord healed her instantly.

The baby's mother could feel the fever leave and never forgot that her little girl was healed in answer to a prayer in Jesus' name. Later, when that little girl was growing up, her mother told her this story many times. When that little girl grew up and married, she gave birth to a little boy whom she named Vital. During Vital's childhood his mother told him this story again and again—making him curious to know who Jesus was.

Now, a high school student in Pandharkawda, Vital attended meetings conducted by Umri Hospital Gospel Teams. When Wesley befriended Vital, his interest had grown enough for him to ask, "How do I become a Christian?"

When shown the way of salvation, he accepted Christ and was given the Christian name, Vijay, meaning victory.

BELL FAMILY NEWS

Chimes, April 1966, gives this glimpse into our lives at that time. "The Umri Bells are having a hard time chiming these days. Why? The daytime temperature is well over 100 degrees, and the nights are hot and stuffy with only occasional relief.

"Even so, the desk work never comes to an end, and Gordon will be staying on through April. Lola and the Dr. Fidler family will soon escape to cool Kodaikanal by train. In case you haven't heard, Gordon is helping with Umri Hospital administration. At the same time, he carries on the work of mission treasurer, as well as other mission business. Lola is getting more practice typing letters, is official packer for our many short trips, prepares flannelgraph stories for our village preaching and manages our household affairs."

Lola's role has always been a very important one. Her advice and encouragement were always invaluable. She declared that she didn't like mathematics and felt she lacked skills in that area. On the other hand, her eye for details often spotted my mistakes in bookkeeping. Nevertheless, she found life more and more difficult, because G.E. and Larry were far off in the United States, while Wes and Verle were a thousand miles away in boarding school.

The above Chimes gave this little report concerning the boys. "G.E. is finishing his second year in Seattle Pacific College–Larry his first. Wesley has one year left in high school before leaving for college–Verle has two."

A recent visit from Dr. Frank Kline gave us news with a little more detail than letters usually give. Larry was doing well enough in his college work, from our point of view. In his mind was the concern that his grades were not good enough to keep him out of the military. At this stage he was seriously thinking that it was better to enlist than to be drafted. We were not fully aware of his thoughts and were too far away to jointly consider the matter or to give him good support. He joined the U.S. Air Force in July 1966.

Dr. Elmer Parsons was known to have some expertise in evaluating conditions and making recommendations for improvement. Dr. Parsons visited Wun, Umri and Yavatmal, spending about a month assessing conditions on our field. He made recommendations regarding ways to proceed with the work. Dr. Parsons led the sessions of the 1966 India

Annual Conference. His messages acknowledged the difficulties we faced but encouraged us to be optimistic about the future.

TEACHING AT U.B.S.

The situation at Umri Hospital no longer required Gordon's help. Dr. Fidler, along with his staff, was now able to manage affairs there. The dean at Union Biblical Seminary came to Gordon with an urgent plea for him to join the teaching staff from November to March. Garden Bungalow would provide good living quarters and office space. Mission business would be more conveniently carried on from Yavatmal. These factors, along with the urgent request from the Seminary, were enough to convince us. We moved back to Garden Bungalow in Yavatmal.

In a letter written April 1967, are these words, "Teaching was like a refresher course. What a blessing to teach young men and women who are eager to learn. Gordon enjoyed the experience. The school year at Union Biblical Seminary ended the first week of March. In fact, Bishop Kendall was here and conducted the India Free Methodist Annual Conference during exam week."

Big changes happened after Christmas in 1966. Serious problems at Kodai School resulted in the closing of two evangelical, boarding homes. A place for Wes and Verle was available at the Nazarene home, but Lola was required to serve as housemother from January to June 1967. For that reason, when the boys went back to school, Lola went with them and took charge of their boarding home for that period.

That year Bishop Kendall stayed with Gordon at Garden Bungalow. Lola was in the hills. Probably the good Bishop noticed the lack of a woman's touch in his entertainment. The Roots were in town and Loretta helped out with suggestions. One of the special privileges Gordon and Lola enjoyed was entertaining denominational leaders from time to time in their home. Among these were Dr. Kirkpatrick, Bishop and Mrs. Paul Ellis, as well as Bishop Cryderman.

From the April, 1967 letter, were these paragraphs:

"Gordon was elected District Superintendent of the Western District. Pray that in spite of language barriers the Holy Spirit will do a work through him.

"Lola has completed her stint as 'Boarding House Mother' and has moved with Wes and Verle to our F.M. house in Blackburn, where Gordon will join them in May.

"A place in an evangelical boarding home has opened for Verle. This will provide for his last year. We thank the Lord for this solution to the boarding problem."

WESLEY GRADUATES FROM HIGH SCHOOL

For the first time Gordon and Lola were able to have a part in the graduation of one of their sons from Kodai School. The junior–senior banquet and the baccalaureate service were pleasant, memorable events. Wesley had done well with his clarinet lessons and had a part in the musical concerts.

From Chimes, November 1967:

"Commencement was a grand occasion. We felt proud that Wes had completed the work required to earn his diploma. To be present and have some part in the graduations celebrations for one of our boys, was a special joy. We had felt equally proud in previous years when G.E. and Larry had worked hard and earned their diplomas. Not being present for their graduations had been equally painful for them and for us."

From a letter dated April, 1967 I quote, "Wesley will graduate from high school on May 9 He plans to leave India about May 20 and to arrive in U.S.A. by the first of

June. He has been accepted at Spring Arbor College for next fall. Pray for summer employment so that he can earn money for college."

The above letter did not tell the following story. A day or two after Wes graduated, we began a tour of South India. The first stop was an Indian National Park called Periar. After renting a motorboat and hiring a guide, we set out to explore the lake and view the wildlife on its shores. Not far from the shore we were rewarded by seeing a large herd of elephants. Standing alone in another valley, we spotted a rogue elephant. What a giant animal he was! To get a better glimpse of him, we had the guide steer our boat fairly close to him. The elephant heard our motor and made as if to chase us. Not willing to take unnecessary chances, we sped away from there.

After spending the night in park lodging, we traveled on to Donavur Fellowship. We had read Amy Carmichael's books and knew some of her story. What a privilege to spend some time on the compound of the institution which she founded. Her followers and the ones who were carrying on her work made gracious arrangements for our stay overnight and gave us a splendid tour with some explanation and history of the work.

The next day we pushed on to the southern most tip of India, Cape Comorin, a most interesting vantage point, where the waters of the Arabian Sea meet the waters of the Bay of Bengal. Wes and Verle took a dip in the warm waters. We enjoyed the delicious lunch prepared for us by the friends at Donovur and pushed on toward the city of Trivandrum in the province of Kerala.

Our dear friends, the Sorbos, had given us their address and invited us to use their empty house for our stay in Trivandrum. The facilities of a beautiful home, with the help of their devoted servants, gave us accommodations far more suitable than a luxury hotel would have been. We spent two days there. Daily, we enjoyed swimming off the famous Kovalam beach not far from Sorbos's home. Swimming in warm, ocean water, being buoyed by gentle, but powerful waves, was a delightful experience.

After two days in Trivandrum it was time for Wes to catch his airplane at Cochin. A city up the coast about 175 miles. An early start got us to the airport in time to see Wes on his plane and on his way back to America, a sad parting, as are all partings from loved ones. A special memory of that parting was seeing Wesley shaking hands with his beloved dog, Buff, as he said a last goodbye.

Now three of our boys were gone from us back to our native land, leaving only our youngest, Verle, to have one more year with us in India. At this stage G. E. was completing his third year at Seattle Pacific College and Larry was studying the Chinese language in the Air Force at Monterey, California.

The next morning after Wes's departure, we started on the return trip to Kodaikanal. We had been urged to be sure to eat some famous fish curry in a restaurant at Cochin. That morning we arranged to do that and will always remember that delicious meal. Lola, however, can't forget the dirty white tablecloth.

Returning to Kodai we approached from a back way. The roads were not as well developed as the more popular route up the mountain. Extensive tea plantations captured our notice, along with other spectacular scenery. At the same time the road challenged us with some, very steep climbs. Lola found some of this difficult. To make it easier for herself, she closed her eyes and tried to sleep in the back seat. An interesting bridge loomed before us, consisting simply of two tracks, each about eighteen inches wide. As we gingerly crossed that bridge, Verle remarked, "It's a good thing Mom is asleep." As it happened, she was awake, but very glad she didn't know what was happening until we had crossed over.

Soon we were back in Kodai. One of the exotic experiences of our lives quickly faded into memory, and we were back to reality. Time had come for Verle to go back to school and for us to return to Yavatmal.

JUNE TO NOVEMBER 1967

The Western District of our India Conference has twenty-four towns and villages in which Christian families live. Previously we visited the towns where pastors live. Now that the rains are over, our goal is to visit every village where Christians live. This goal, along with mission treasurer's work and other mission business, promises to keep us busy.

"Lola has been helping in Yavatmal with Womens Missionary Society projects and Sunday school classes. One class on Saturday and two Sunday morning classes combined include more than one hundred children. She has also been active in a regular Sunday evening ministry to Christian nurses in local hospitals. She is thankful to the Lord for these avenues of service.

"We were overjoyed, three years ago, when Vijay Siddam gave his heart to Christ. After a time he brought his new wife to us. Together they took their stand in Christian baptism. We were thrilled again when his mother and father joined them. Thus the whole family stood for Christ in Sunna.

"Opposition arose in the village. They were refused water from the community well. People threatened and abused them. The mother endured beating at the hands of other women in her caste. Their testimony was, 'Though they kill us we will not give up Christ.' "

Also included in that November Chimes was the following:

"G.E. is a senior at Seattle Pacific College this year. He is talking of marriage soon. It looks like we might welcome that first daughter into the family before long.

"Larry completed the Chinese language course in May. He returned to an airbase in Texas where he has completed several short courses related to his Air Force duties. He is currently transferring to Spokane, Washington, for some flight training before he goes overseas.

"Wesley found a happy home for the summer with Lola's niece and family in Detroit. With their help he landed a job almost immediately, and was able to save enough to enter Spring Arbor College in September.

"Verle arrived home for Christmas vacation today. We look forward to two happy months with

him now and a few rushed days with him in May before he, too, shall fly away to U.S.A. THANK YOU FOR YOUR PRAYERS ON BEHALF OF THE BOYS."

FINAL MONTHS OF FIRST PERIOD WITH THE FREE METHODIST MISSION

In January of 2003, I am looking back and recording my recollections. Important events took place that were not written either in Chimes or other letters at the time, which I am compelled to include here. Some of the happenings were indelibly written on my mind. Inevitably what I write will be from my own point of view.

We spent seven years in India before joining the Free Methodist Mission. This made possible a perspective that combined experience in another mission together with what we were seeing in the Free Methodist Mission. Hence, we were not boxed in by an exclusive Free Methodist mindset.

Things were very rapidly progressing to the place where Lola and I were to take over the major responsibility of mission leadership. We had seen some things which we felt needed to be considered. For the most part, our point of view was not even under consideration. Mission leaders were about to turn all responsibilities over to us without sitting down with us and seriously giving thought to our point of view about the future.

One significant consideration, in our point of view, was being overlooked. We had an important observation in the previous mission, which was reinforced in the Free Methodist work. Converts to Christianity were almost all from low caste or outcaste people in villages. After these people responded to the gospel, they were no longer content to continue living as coolies for the landlords. Over a period of time, they migrated to larger towns or industrial cities in search of jobs. In time, entire village congregations disappeared. All had left for better circumstances. For example, one of the congregations of another denomination in Bombay was found to be actually made up largely of Free Methodist people.

My contention was that we needed a two-pronged approach to the work. Without abandoning our rural emphasis, we needed to follow our people to the major cities and plant urban as well as rural churches. My argument was that failure to do so would result in supplying other denominations with members while slowly losing our own. I brought up these matters in private discussion. No official response ever came from the older missionaries or from the denominational leaders who came to view the work and conduct the annual conferences, unless what is written below was that response.

Dr. Charles Kirkpatrick came to India in February of 1968. He met with the senior missionaries, and together they drew some conclusions. On one occasion I was sent off to Nagpur on an errand. When I returned, I walked into a meeting that was taking place. As I walked in, I heard Dr. Kirkpatrick making a pronouncement, based upon the older missionaries' viewpoint. He declared that the Lord had assigned Yavatmal District to our mission and that we must confine our work to that assignment.

Could it be that they were so insensitive that they weren't aware of what they were doing? Didn't they know that the one who was being called upon to carry out these orders was not included in the deliberations? Or, was it possible that they deliberately did it this way in order to hand me an ultimatum without asking for my input? I think I could have accepted a decision coming from a democratic process. If my position had been adequately presented and was dulyoutvoted, I think I could have handled that. This kind of dictatorial pronouncement was very disturbing to me.

As the story unfolds, the reader will discover that my displeasure and protest were not in vain. Eventually a new outlook resulted in a very positive outcome.

VERLE'S GRADUATION AND DEPARTURE WITH LOLA TO THE U.S.

Dr. Demaray, along with Dr. Kirkpatrick visited India at this time. Frank and Betty Kline had encouraged G.E. and his fiancee, Mary Kurtti, to get married right after G.E.'s graduation. That way Lola could accompany Verle to the States, attend the graduation and wedding and then see Verle established in college. This was discussed with Dr. Demaray and the whole matter approved by Dr. Kirkpatrick.

Verle was a member of the school choir and was hopeful that we could be present for the choir's concert, along with all the other events surrounding his graduation. For that reason we left for the hills a little earlier than usual. For the second time, we had the joy of being present for the important events centered around one of our son's graduation from high school. The details were similar to those already described for Wesley's graduation. Without being repetitious, let us say that these were pleasantly sweet days, to be forever remembered. Like the exquisite blossom of a rose, they are too soon over, though not forgotten.

A letter written from Niles, Michigan February 12, 1969 gives some of the details:

"Verle, our youngest son, graduated from Kodaikanal High School in May, 1968. A few days later, Lola and Verle flew from India to Okinawa, where they visited with Larry. Larry is stationed there in the Security Division of the Air Force.

"Even though Larry could not plan on free time to visit, we felt that it miraculously worked out for a two-day visit with him. Then flying on to Seattle, Lola and Verle visited with Gordon's Mother and other relatives and friends who were there. (His father passed away in 1967.) Verle went on to Detroit, after a few days, to find a job. Lola stayed in Seattle for Gordon Elvan's graduation and wedding.

"Work did not turn up for Verle in Detroit. For that reason Lola went as quickly as she could to arrange something for him and for herself. They went to Spring Arbor, where Wesley had spent the previous year in College. Gracious friends in the Spring Arbor Church and in the College helped them to find living quarters and employment. Wesley and Verle were able to live with their Mom for the summer and for the first semester of college. Lola's Mother joined them at that time, too.

"Gordon stayed on in India to carry on the work. Rev. and Mrs. Root had gone on furlough. Though due for retirement, they returned to India in November. For Gordon, it was a long, lonely, six months without the family, but with more than plenty to do to keep busy.

"On the way home, Gordon stopped off in Palestine for four days. He had a delightful time, visiting Jerusalem, Jericho, the Dead Sea, Bethlehem, Samaria, Hebron and other sights. His only regret was that he did not have two weeks instead of four days. A longer stay, when Lola was not with him, was unthinkable.

"G.E. and his wife Mary work for the school department of Cleveland, Ohio. This made it possible for them to visit us at Thanksgiving and again at Christmas time. We were only sorry that Larry could not join us from Okinawa.

"We do not feel led to return to the work in India for reasons which cannot be explained in detail here. Suffice it to say that we believe our particular contribution to the work was completed. For that reason we accepted an appointment to the Free Methodist Church in Niles, Michigan."

The reader will connect the thoughts of the last paragraph above with what I wrote earlier. However, that decision was reconsidered later on.

As it turned out, we did not return to India for more than five years. In actual fact, at this time in her life, Lola could not have endured staying in India any longer. Both physical and psychological causes left her in a state of deep depression. She could not have endured total separation from our children any longer. Added to this was the fact that her Mother needed to live with us for her final years. These are some of the reasons we did not return to India in the normal period of time.

FIVE YEARS IN AMERICA

Hillsdale Free Methodist Church had become our home church. God gave us many wonderful friends in that congregation. Harry Bonney, pastor of the church at that time, came to know that we were leaving India for an extended period. He invited us to join his staff. That was a generous offer and tempting for us to consider. After prayer and consideration we felt led to decline this offer in favor of a small pastorate.

Rev. Dale Cryderman, superintendent of the Southern Michigan Conference, offered us the pastorate in Niles, Michigan. A student pastor was due to return to school in January. We were appointed to take over from January 1, 1969.

The parsonage proved to be a wonderful provision for our need. A bedroom downstairs was just right for Lola's mother. A little plumbing turned a small room into a bathroom for her, providing adequate accommodations for Lola's mother on the ground floor. The upstairs had three bedrooms and bath–accommodations for us, and for family or friends to come and visit. We were so glad that during the next summer Wesley and Verle could live with us while they worked to save money for school.

The congregation had a lovely new church building five miles across town from the parsonage. The new building was financed by the Free Methodist Denomination as part of a church-planting project. A bit of the history leading up to this will help to explain the situation we found.

Free Methodists were invited to take over the congregation and the property of a work that Reverend and Mrs. Culp had established on the eastern edge of the city of Niles. The property included a parsonage and an older wooden frame church building. Over a period of time, the Free Methodist pastor, working with conference leadership, decided to sell the old church building and build a new building on the opposite side of the city. The idea was to move from a blue-collar neighborhood to an area with middle and upper middle class homes. In effect, the people, who formerly belonged to Reverend and Mrs. Culp's congregation, chose not to attend the new church across town. In addition it proved to be difficult to attract people to form a completely new congregation to fill a new building in a new part of town.

We found a little group, who because of their Free Methodist backgrounds, faithfully attended each Sunday. The impressive building caused people to check us out from timeto time. What they found was a lovely sanctuary with very few people attending. Young couples in the congregation with growing families had experienced this situation for some time and worried about the future. If the congregation did not grow, would there be a youth fellowship for their young people?

Churches in the conference were willing to help. Spring Arbor and Hillsdale churches, among others, sent musical teams and special speakers. We advertised these special programs and tried to promote interest with much visitation. Sometimes the guest teams were almost more in number than the people who turned out. In fact, people turned out better when talent within the congregation took part.

We did our best and worked diligently as well as prayed earnestly. Growth was very slow. At the General Conference in 1969, our conference superintendent was elected Bishop. A new superintendent was elected to fill that vacancy. Soon after his election the new man felt he must take some action regarding the work at Niles. We do not know what pressures were upon him to make the decisions he made.

PASTORAL TESTING TIMES

In the spring of 1970, we were notified that we would soon need to store our furniture in a moving van and move out of the parsonage. The superintendent was appointing another more aggressive man, a professor from a college in Kalamazoo, to pastor the church. He would live in his own home. This would release the parsonage to be sold and some of the indebtedness on the new building could be paid off.

This news was a little difficult for us handle, for a number of reasons. Lola's mother was in a nursing home in Niles. Her condition would not permit her to be moved. We were given no word concerning an appointment elsewhere. Basically we were facing, at the very least, being temporarily without a home and without employment, but the Lord's timing was perfect, as always.

As it turned out, Mrs. Kelley, Lola's mother, passed away on June 17, 1970 Before we had to make the move, the funeral service for Lola's mother was held. It took place at the funeral home in Hillsdale, Michigan. She was laid to rest a few miles south and east of Hillsdale in Maple Grove Cemetery. After spending some time with Lola's relatives, who had gathered for the funeral, we returned to Niles and vacated the parsonage.

Our second son, Larry had returned from Okinawa with his bride Kimi and was serving the last of his military assignment in Omaha, Nebraska. We decided to make the trip to Omaha to meet his new bride and spend a few days near them. Looking back, we are grateful for this slot of time that was open for this important visit.

At the 1970 Annual Conference we were appointed to serve at Pulaski Free Methodist Church. Pulaski is located about twelve miles west and south of Spring Arbor, Michigan. In many ways this appointment proved to be ideal for us. Working with country people in a beautiful rural setting was just what we wanted. In addition, we were to enjoy a lovely new parsonage and a modest church building free of indebtedness.

During the next four years we learned to love the people. We made some very dear friends who have kept in touch with us through the years. In addition, family members came to visit us quite often. Financially our living was hand-to-mouth, but in many other ways we were richly rewarded for our labor. There were some rough spots, but over all we think of these as very pleasant years of our lives.

To help our financial situation Lola worked as a teacher's aide in the Concord Public School. From time to time

I worked in Mr. Park's box factory at Spring Arbor. In the course of four years at Pulaski, we were able to see some improvements made to the church property. A concrete floor was poured in the garage. A rough basement in the parsonage was finished and turned into a beautiful fellowship hall. Improvements were made to the parking lot including lighting and a sidewalk from the places of parking to the church entrance.

A CALL TO RETURN TO INDIA

In our fourth year at Pulaski, the Department of World Mission contacted us. Rev. Elmer Parsons called asking if perhaps this was the time for us to return to the field. He spoke of a response-taking place among the tribal people. Officials felt that our leadership would be valuable in the situation. Our reply was that we would think and pray about it and let them know our decision later.

We had seventy young couples on our prospect list for Pulaski Free Methodist Church. We felt that a younger pastor could more effectively reach out to these couples as well as organize a more effective youth ministry. This feeling seemed in agreement with the call to return to India.

We were privileged to enjoy one last major event with the Pulaski congregation. They celebrated their twenty-fifth anniversary, a special day in the life of the church.

Visas to India were only being granted to missionaries who had a special expertise needed by the church in India. We believed the best thing for us to do was to go back as a teacher at Union Biblical Seminary in Yavatmal. We were also certain that the principal, Dr. Saphir Athyal, would insist that anyone teaching on his staff must have at least a master's degree in some subject.

With this thought in mind, I contacted the General Missionary Board and said that we would consider going back to India providing they sponsored a year at Fuller Theological Seminary to study for a master's degree. Dr. Charles Kirkpatrick, Mission Secretary at that time, agreed to this proposal. We were soon under appointment to return to India after a year at Fuller.

Asbury Theological Seminary had a good School of Mission. I might have chosen to go there to earn a master's degree. The School of World Mission at Fuller was better known. I had also been impressed with the writings of Dr. Donald McGavran. An important reason, however, for choosing Fuller was the desire to spend some time near Larry, Kimi and family.

Going back to school at fifty-two years of age was a major decision. It required selling all of our furniture and reducing our belongings to fit into a small luggage trailer. As always, the breaking-up of housekeeping and getting ready for a major move was more difficult for Lola than for me. But, as usual, she handled the challenge with courage and prepared to support me in my effort to earn a master's degree.

Our little trailer had very small wheels and a rather insubstantial frame to carry the heavy load we put upon it. To avoid possible problems we bought an extra wheel and tire as well as an extra bearing in case one burned out on the trip. Surprisingly, the little trailer developed no problems along the way.

In order to reduce hotel and motel expenses, we purchased a small tent and planned to stop at KOA camping spots on the journey. Avoiding hotels or motels for two nights would have paid for the tent. Good weather, near Oklahoma City, gave us a pleasant night in the tent. The next night, in the high lands of New Mexico, was too chilly for sleeping out. The following night, it seemed obvious that a night in the lower altitude of Arizona would be dry and convenient to use our tent. Instead, heavy rains were falling. Because flash floods made the roads unsafe for travel, we spent another night in a motel.

The last leg of our journey would take us over several hundred miles of Arizona and California desert. Late July was the very hottest time of the year. Every effort was made to be ready for this part of the trip. The car was thoroughly checked to be quite sure it was ready for the test. Extra water supply was provided. To avoid the terrific daytime heat, plans were made to travel at night.

When signs of increasing population began to appear east of Los Angeles, we felt a tremendous relief. At least there would be help available in case of car trouble or whatever. Even at mid-morning the temperature was soaring. We had no air-conditioning in the car. It remained very hot most of the way, but the temperature moderated somewhat by the time we arrived at San Diego. The good news was that nights were pleasantly cool and comfortable for sleeping.

Larry, Kimi and family received us warmly. We made plans to visit until the weekend, when Larry could go with us and help us find housing in Pasadena. Their son Ernie was four years old and their daughter Emily two at that time.

Needless to say, we enjoyed the children as well as having a good visit with Larry and Kimi.

On Saturday, with Larry's help as a guide, we easily found Fuller Seminary. Their staff gave information that helped us find a lovely apartment within walking distance of the seminary. Providentially we were quite early and found accommodations readily available.

A YEAR AT FULLER

What a privilege to go back to school and to study under outstanding professors. I was to study subjects directly related to missionary work. To have learned many of these things years earlier, when we first began as missionaries, would have been so helpful. At least I had the privilege to learn them then.

Lola helped me in whatever way she could. She needed to get training that would make her time on the field more meaningful and challenging. She was interested in library work and was hired at a library in the neighborhood. She also enrolled in library science classes at Pasadena Community College.

The year went by very quickly. In addition to a full academic load, we found time for fun things. Larry and Kimi came to visit us several times and we went to visit them. Gordon and Mary with the children came down to see the Rose Parade and all of us went to Disneyland. By God's grace, Lola and I did well in our studies and were better prepared to return to India and to serve at Union Biblical Seminary.

Larry and Kimi came with Ernie and Emily for my graduation in 1975. A little incident, during the graduation exercises, stands out in our memories. I was walking across the platform to receive my diploma when young Ernie called out, "There goes Grandpa!"

Verle came down for that occasion as well. The next day he joined Lola and me on a trip to Yosemite National Park. What a great way to celebrate my graduation! Walking amongst the giant sequoia trees was a moving experience. Standing at the foot of an ancient tree, hundreds of years old and hundreds of feet tall, made one feel very close to God who created such a marvelous world and universe.

Lola and I packed up and moved to San Diego to spend a few weeks near Larry and Kimi before we left for India. We found a small room in a rooming house not far from Larry's home. Extra special to us at that time was a visit from my brother Leonard, his wife Ann and family who came all the way from Michigan. Of course, they did many other things on that trip, but we were glad to be included. My brother Warren and his wife Elaine came down at the same time. This sparked a mini family reunion.

Two things needed to happen before we could start our journey back to India. The monsoons had to cool down the weather in India, and certain equipment must be located and purchased. Two of the major items were a special kind of Maytag washing machine and an electric stove. To locate what we wanted and get them crated and shipped took some time.

Finally the time had come to serve again with the Department of World Missions of the Free Methodist Church. We had been away from India from January 1969 to July 1974, a little more than five and a half years!

BACK TO INDIA IN 1975

Our preparations completed, we said farewell to Larry's family and made the trip to Seattle. At that time Gordon and Mary were living in Poulsbo. After a few days with them, they took us to Vancouver, British Columbia where we boarded a Japanese Airline flight via Tokyo and Bangkok to Bombay.

Dr. & Mrs. Williams, and some of our friends from Umri Hospital and Yavatmal Seminary met us at Nagpur airport. What a delightful way to be welcomed back. On the trip from Nagpur to Yavatmal, we found the Wardha River at flood stage–a vivid reminder that monsoons were very active. After spending a somewhat difficult night in Wardha, we travelled on to Yavatmal the next day.

A large apartment, in Baptist House on the seminary compound was fully furnished and waiting for us with both flowers and vegetables in the garden. A minimum of settling in was required, for which we were very, very grateful. These and other gestures of love towards us will forever be appreciated.

THE LATTER YEARS OF MISSION SERVICE

Lola very quickly became involved in library work. In January 1976, we wrote, "Book mending occupies much of Lola's time. She has recently set up shop on our verandah so that she can answer the door and attend to other household matters while repairing a constant flow of worn books and putting them back into circulation."

Missionaries typically wear many hats. This sometimes results in one becoming "jack of all trades and master of none." In the above letter were these words, "Gordon is part-time teacher, enjoying his class in Biblical Backgrounds. He is part-time evangelist, going out nearly every weekend."

Also, as is usual for a missionary, he served in many ways: on the Umri Hospital Board of Directors, a member of the Conference Executive Committee, on the Board of Governors of Union Biblical Seminary, and a member of the Mission Executive Committee.

In addition to these duties, tribal evangelism began to emerge as one of the most challenging opportunities on the field. Rev. T. L. Naik and Rev. V.S. Sidam were the Indian workers assigned to this ministry. Because of the growing potential in this ministry, Dr. Charles Kirkpatrick, Missionary Secretary, wished to prepare a moving picture presenting the work. Dr. Victor Macy, who had done a number of films for the General Mission Board, would come to produce this moving picture. We were privileged to work with Dr. Macy and his wife Susan in producing this film, which Dr. Macy decided to name "Bridges to God."

The story in that film is part of our history and bears telling in our personal record.

BRIDGES TO GOD

As already mentioned, Rev. T. L. Naik and Rev. Vijay Sidam were appointed as my co-workers for tribal evangelism. (Henceforth referred to as Naik and Sidam.) The reader will remember the Sidam story earlier in our journal. Sidam went on to receive training at Chikalda Lay Leaders' School under the direction of Rev. Elmer S. Root. After completing his training, he joined my team as an evangelist to the tribal people. Naik was formerly one of the instructors at the Lay Leaders' School. Later he had been appointed by Rev. Root to work in the Kolamb tribe.

Aborigines throughout India were exploited by conquering races. Some of them became slave laborers for those who conquered them. Anthropologists believe that these people became the outcast peoples of India. Others refused to succumb to such slavery and fled deeper into the forests and higher in the hills. These are the fiercely independent, tribal people found in the reserve forests and remote hills of India. One such group is the Kolambs.

India's central government passed laws permitting these tribal people to occupy land in the reserve forests. The Mangs, as already mentioned, were trying to drive the Kolambs off their rightful territory and take it for themselves. We decided to change our focus from trying to work with the Mang people and to work with the Kolambs. From our earliest years at Adilabad, we had been interested in these tribal people. Finally the time had come when a ministry could be started among them. Naik had returned to the field and was ready to begin work.

Reports of an outstanding response to the gospel in the Hirapur area had come to the Free Methodist Mission Board in the United States. This reported response led to Lola and me being requested to return to India and help organize the discipling of these people. The report said that 1,200 people had accepted baptism. Quite likely, these people responded with a minimum of understanding. We had no problem with this. Even if their commitment was shallow, a friendliness to the Gospel would give us a wide open door for teaching them and discipling them for Christ. With that in mind we returned to the field and were ready to begin work.

Accompanied by Naik, Sidam and a young man named Namawad, we traveled to Hirapur to check out the facts. The response was reportedly from the Mang caste. Mr. Namawad being from that group of people hoped to be assigned to minister to them. We asked Mr. Namawad to introduce us to some of the 1,200 people who were supposed to be baptised converts. To make a long story short, after considerable time and repeated visits among his people, he was not able to introduce us to a single convert. Mr. Namawad had every reason to make his best effort to show us these people because his future employment depended upon it. The fact is that he never was able to show us any evidence that there was a single bona fide convert out of the reported 1,200.

Delving further into the matter, we found some answers to the mystery. Hirapur was located in government monitored, reserve forest territory. These Mang people were encroaching in an area assigned to tribal people. They were being ordered by government authorities to vacate this area. Someone led them to believe that missionaries could influence the authorities to change their mind. When they found out that missionaries would not get involved in their battle, their friendliness turned to anger. To our disappointment, instead of finding a friendly people ready to be discipled for Christ, we found people who were hostile to us. Instead of a wide open door, we found one tightly shut.

With the door closed to ministry among the Mangs, we were now free to turn to the Ghonds. From our earliest years at Adilabad, we had been interested in these tribal people. Finally the time had come when a ministry could be started among them. Naik had worked with these people for some time and had reduced some of their language to writing.

The two men, Naik and Sidam, began to make regular visits to the Hirapur area. Sometimes they camped in their villages for two weeks or more at a time. From time to time I joined them for a few days. In our January 1976, letter we wrote, "Gordon went to join the team in Hirapur on December 27 and stayed until January 1. He walked over 100 miles in two visits and fell in love with those hills. What is more important, he found several groups of people who were hungry to be taught."

Over a period of time Naik and Sidam visited quite a few of the surrounding tribal villages and talked with the chiefs and elders in these villages. One of Gordon's visits was at a time when the chiefs and elders from nearly a dozen villages gathered to talk about becoming Christians. They had some interesting questions for which they wanted answers. Here are two of the major questions:

If our sons become Christians, where will they find women to marry?

If we become Christians, do we give up all of our tribal customs?

We had discussed these important matters in workers' conferences and were prepared to give the people answers. In response to the first question, we told them that we were not expecting them to come one by one. Instead we hoped that they would come by families and even by whole villages. Grandparents, parents, children, relatives and extended families could all decide to become Christians together. We knew that this was their social pattern. We wanted them make a decision in the way their culture required.

In answer to the second question, we told them that they would be Kolamb Christians. They need not change any of their customs except those that the Bible clearly said were wrong. We were careful to let them know that we would help them study the Bible and make decisions on the basis of their own understanding of what the scriptures taught.

An example of the kind of thing we needed to think through follows. One day I arrived at Hirapur and was shocked to see the men all sitting in a Gospel meeting with their headgear on. Naik and Sidam would have had plenty of time to teach the people about our Christian customs by now. I turned to Naik and Sidam and asked, "Why do they have their hats on?" At the close of the service they explained that the Kolamb custom is to put the hat on in the presence of important people and in worship. This is their cultural way of expressing honor and respect. After some discussion, we decided to let them keep their hats on in a worship service. After they read the Bible for themselves they may decide on their own to change this custom.

Several months passed until, under the leadership of the chief, all of the Kolambs in the village of Hirapur made a decision to become Christians. In addition, there were people in surrounding villages who were showing interest.

Animism is the basic religious background for these people. They live in constant fear of the demons that are believed to inhabit the atmosphere around their village. They now began to have faith that the power of Christ was greater than the power of the demons. They saw demons cast out through prayers of faith and their faith was strengthened. In time the people began to feel the need for a place to worship. One of the farmers offered his house to be turned into a Christian house of worship. A weekend was set aside to dedicate the church and to celebrate certain Christian rites. Naik and Sidam arranged for me to be present for the occasion.

Now the rainy season was over, the dirt roads, and small streams had dried up, traveling to Hirapur in the Jeep station wagon was now possible. I arrived at the village early on Friday evening. Naik and Sidam had arranged for me to camp with them in a large metal building about a quarter of a mile from the village. I set up my cot and prepared my evening meal. Naik and Sidam explained that because the tribals had major plans for the next day and were busy with preparations, no night meeting was planned. We were free to read, rest or visit.

They intended that the things they were planning should be a surprise to me. Since I had no idea what they planned, I was not as excited as I might have been. That helped me to get a good night's sleep. Awaking before sunrise, I had devotions and prepared breakfast. Naik and Sidam left me alone in the corrugated tin shed and went off to help the tribals finalize their preparations.

I was alone deep in the hills of the Federal Reserve Forest on a crystal clear morning. Except for the occasional cooing of turtle-doves, bird calls and a few jungle sounds, the morning was conspicuously quiet. It was as if the evil schemes of the village demons had been quashed by the Holy Spirit. The resulting peace and calm was so real one could almost reach out and touch it. I found myself waiting in a silence that seemed to be saying, "Be alert for something remarkable is about to happen."

THE GRAND CEREMONY BEGINS!

Suddenly, in the midst of that stark silence, it was as if bombs burst in the morning air. The tribals began to beat their drums and blow their horns. The door of my tin house looked

directly out upon the road that led to the village. There, marching up the road toward me were the drummers and musicians, leading a parade. Almost the entire village population followed behind. What a never-to-be-forgotten sight and experience.

Arriving at my door, they requested that I drive the Jeep station wagon and follow the native orchestra back to the village. They further requested that many of them be permitted to ride in the Jeep as part of the grand procession. Perhaps twenty or thirty children and young people managed to climb into or onto the Jeep and ride slowly in the procession. Those who could not ride marched along in front, beside or in back of the Jeep while the musicians led the way back down the road to the village.

At the entrance of the village a bamboo-laticed archway had been erected. Green-leafed twigs and some native flowers were woven into the lattice, giving a very impressive appearance. One had a feeling of grandeur passing through the archway and on into the village.

The procession came to a stop at the first village hut on the right side of the road. This was the house that had been donated for a place of worship. After seating for Naik, Sidam and me were provided, the people gathered around, and the service of dedication began.

A crude pulpit with a cross on its front had been constructed. Also two or three simple benches made up the sum total of the furniture. As many people as could find space sat on mats in the center of the room. Others squatted, in typical Indian fashion, around the edges of the room or just outside the door.

The ceremony was simple with every effort to teach from Scripture important principles for them to learn. The reading was from Psalm 127:1 "Except the Lord build the house, they labor in vain that build it." When the service was over, the chief and village elders said, "Now we know what to do."

After this service was over and some time had elapsed, the people said, "One of our men passed away since we became Christians. We buried our friend, but we want to have a Christian ceremony on his behalf." After some discussion, a time was set for early afternoon to gather at the graveside and have a funeral service.

These events were important history-making, precedent-setting events for the people of this tribe. This was the first congregation to be established for this particular ethnic group. Foundations were being laid for church planting throughout the tribe. More than 55,000 people might very well turn from their heathen idols to the Lord Jesus Christ. Everything we did had significance, not just for this day and this event, but also for many such days and events in the future. How very important that we have the direction of the Lord and that the foundations be laid carefully!

A crude wooden cross was prepared to plant at the head of the grave. Again a simple ceremony was conducted using appropriate Scripture from I Corinthians 15 and especially the words of Jesus in John 11:25, "I am the resurrection, and the life: he that believeth in me, though he were dead, yet shall he live: and whosoever liveth and believeth in me shall never die." Both Naik and Sidam gave appropriate thoughts for the occasion. The people found a new peace and closure as the result of this service. Again the leaders said, "Now we know what to do."

We knew that Kolambs had harvest festivals. These people, who formerly had a practice of honoring their heathen gods at harvest time, needed to have a functional substitute appropriate for Christians. The people decided they would gather the next morning at the "threshing floor" of the village chief and have a ceremony of thanksgiving and praise to God for His bountiful blessings.

The threshing floor is in the form of a round circle about fifteen to twenty feet in diameter. The chief laid corn stocks around the edge of the circle. The ground of the floor had been carefully pounded and plastered. All cracks in the area were filled that no grain would disappear into the deep cracks in the ground. The chief poured grain, about three inches deep, to cover the entire floor. Then, a cross was formed out of corn stalks and laid on top of the grain to provide clear symbolism for our Christian ceremony.

Naik, Siddam and I had searched the Bible for appropriate Scripture for the occasion. We found help in Deuteronomy

26. It suggested that grain be put in a basket and presented to the Lord. The village chief filled a small basket with grain and lifted it toward heaven while a prayer of thanksgiving was prayed.

The importance of a feast to commemorate the occasion was not forgotten. Feasting, singing and tribal dancing brought a happy climax to this weekend of celebration.

After a time, additional workers became available to carry on the work among the tribal people. Friends Missionary Prayer Band supplied workers for our field. The mission arm of India Evangelical Fellowship sent workers into our area. A graduate from Union Biblical Seminary, Rev. Kulotungan, founded Maharashtra Village Mission. Much of his work has been among tribal people. He is considering bringing churches under the Free Methodist umbrella. The last report indicates eighty tribal congregations affiliated with our work in Maharashtra.

Very recently we have news of an important development. Rev. G. John, a graduate from Union Biblical Seminary, gave his life to tribal evangelism in Andhra State. He has established more than 200 congregations as the fruit of his labors. Rev. John has chosen to bring all of his churches into

Free Methodism. This brings 17,000 adult tribal members and another 6,000 junior members into our denomination.

This is good news in itself. Beyond that, is the potential for sharing of principles and strategies that work. The result could be a greatly expanded response from the tribals in Maharashtra. The potential that is developing in this area of the work is almost beyond imagination. What a thrill to begin seeing this happen in our lifetime!

OTHER MISSIONARY DUTIES

Umri Christian Hospital required much of our time in our last years in India. The major problem was securing doctors. For two years or more we spent half of our week at Yavatmal and half at Umri. The major problem was securing doctors

On more than one occasion we came dangerously close to being forced to shut the doors and finalize the hospital work. The Lord sent in a doctor at the last minute and the work carried on. Through the years hundreds of lives have been saved and thousands of people have found medical help that made a wonderful difference in their lives. Not the least of the good done has been a faithful witness, day after day, to the patients who come. Many of them have found Christ.

Along with other duties, the rather new opportunity in the large city of Bombay began to require time and attention. The unfolding of this new branch of our ministry is an important part of our story.

BOMBAY STORY

Earlier we wrote about the official decision to restrict, for the most part, the work of the Free Methodist Mission in India to Yavatmal District. We expressed our frustration with that decision. After we returned to India in 1975, Rev. Robert Cranston was our Southeast Asia Director. We discussed with him the rationale of extending our work to Bombay. No doubt he discussed this with Dr. Kirkpatrick. In due time we were authorized to recruit someone to start the work in Bombay. Having this door now opened to us brought much joy to our hearts.

Dr. Narendra John, a professor at Union Biblical Seminary, helped recruit one of the more mature students who was open to help us. We remember that he was from Karnatica State, but cannot recall his name. He lived and worked under difficult circumstances, but was successful, in spite of this, in gathering a small nucleus around which a Bombay congregation could be formed.

Living in inhospitable quarters as well as being separated from his family was too much for him and after several months he resigned. We certainly would not criticize him for doing that. Thanks go to him for undertaking the most difficult part of planting the church in Bombay. In addition, he deserves the credit for laying the foundation for the great work that was to follow.

At this time, Rev. V. B. Samudre retired from his position as professor at Union Biblical Seminary. His reputation was known far and wide. He also had relatives in Bombay. He was the right one to lead the congregation through the next step. Rev. Samudre was an older man and limited in the amount of energy he could give to the work. In spite of that, the Lord used him to help establish the new congregation.

Sunday services were being held in the living room of one the families. No suitable housing could be found for the pastor. I was truly sorry and troubled to have Rev. and Mrs Samudre living in very unsuitable quarters. Again and again Rev. Samudre called from Bombay and said, "We have found the right property to buy. Please come and see about it."

Time after time I made the round trip to Bombay hoping to buy a building that would work for a parsonage and temporarily, at least, for worship. Each time I returned without success. The people selling property in Bombay would only give a receipt for half the price paid. I could not accept this way of doing business.

The hot season came. For travel in the hot season, reservations for accommodations on trains, buses or planes, must be scheduled months in advance. For that reason we requested Rev. Samudre not to call us while we were in the hills. Lola and I were just nicely settled in our cottage in the hills, when a telegram came saying, "We have found just the right property. We must make a solid offer in the next 24 hours or we will lose it. Please come."

Remember that getting travel accommodations quickly in the hot season is virtually impossible. When the call came, Lola and I prayed about it. We decided that I should at least try to make the trip to Bombay in 24 hours. Even in the regular season that would be difficult. In the hot season it would be nearly impossible. I really expected to find it impossible and be back home in a few hours. If I made it to Bombay in time, it would be a miracle and a sure sign that the deal in Bombay was the Lord's doing.

The first step was a trip down the mountain on the hill train. I purchased a ticket and took my seat. In a few minutes a train official came and said, "There has been an accident. The track is blocked just a few miles below. The train will not travel for several hours." My first thought was, "My trip to Bombay is finished!" That idea was soon changed. When I went to the station to get a refund for my ticket, two other passengers invited me to share taxi fare to the railway station at the foot hill. I agreed to do this, and we were soon there.

Now came the next test. Almost certainly there would be no chance for reservations on the train to Madras. I went to see the stationmaster. He said, "You're in luck. We have just attached an extra first-class carriage and you can book first class reservations to Madras." Unbelievable and amazing!

That carriage had a flat wheel that bumped and banged all the way to Madras.

I had very little sleep, but I arrived safely in Madras very early in the morning.

One major hurdle still remained. I must catch a plane from Madras to Bombay in order to arrive there on time. Air travel reservations are fully booked weeks in advance. It was almost certain that reservations would not be available in this situation. Considering what had already happened, I couldn't stop at this point. Catching a taxi, I went to the downtown ticket office. There I was told that the situation was worse. The larger airplane that was to make that flight had crashed the night before. A smaller plane was put in its place. Many passengers who had reservations could not get on. .

After a while, the lobby was completely empty. The clerk called me over and whispered a suggestion to me. "Go to the airport. Ask at the window if they will sell you a first-class ticket." Why would an Indian man give me that suggestion? Perhaps he wanted a bribe. I never thought of that. Having come this far, there was no point in not trying. I took a taxi to the airport, went to the clerks at the ticket window and asked, "Will you sell me a first-class ticket?" To my amazement they sold me the ticket. I boarded the plane, when many people with reservations were left behind, and arrived in Bombay in less than 24 hours after the message came. What a miracle!

We negotiated with the company that had the apartment for sale. The deal was completed and the down payment made. This was a nice apartment on the first floor of a large high-rise building. Well worth all the delay we had experienced! This same apartment remains the parsonage for the mother church in Bombay to this very day.

For several years the growing congregation met in the living room of that apartment. They hung an awning over the verandah, just outside the living room, to expand the seating space. In this way they were able to seat seventy people or more. That apartment became the foundation for all of the work that followed. Rev. and Mrs. Samudre were to enjoy this apartment for the last few years of their ministry.

Rev. William John followed the Samudres. This young pastor, under the blessing of the Lord, saw the work in Bombay explode. From one small congregation with fourteen members, the work in Bombay has grown to thirty congregations with nearly two thousand members.

Eventually the Free Methodist Mission in India was able to buy a building that could be renovated and enlarged. Several different groups gather there for worship on Sunday. In addition, a Bible School meets there to train workers for ministry in Bombay. To God be the Glory!

OUR WORK AT UNION BIBLICAL SEMINARY

My having a part in planting a church in Bombay and making treks into the hills to work among tribal people were extra activities having to be done on weekends or during breaks between semesters. Classes at Union Biblical Seminary (UBS) went on regularly.

As one of the mission teachers at the Seminary, I taught Missionary Anthropology and Church Growth Strategy. At this particular time missions was a very popular topic on the campus. This interest resulted in as many as 75 students in my classes.

Because India was formerly a British colony, British ideas about education prevailed in the schools. One of these ideas was the use of essay questions in almost all exams. With many of my students being weak in English and their handwriting very difficult to read, grading 75 exam papers, consisting of essay answers to questions, could be quite a chore. Furthermore some students, unsure of the correct answer, would filibuster. That is, they would write and write to make up for not knowing the correct answer.

Being weak in English posed a problem for many students and for the teachers too. Delivering the full content of the course, for those students capable of receiving it, and at the same time helping the weaker students to get as much as possible out of the course was a challenge. Excellent grades were given only to those students who understood the material and wrote well. For weaker students, considerable allowance had to be made for spelling and grammar. A passing grade was given if there was indication that the student grasped the essential principles and ideas presented in the course. Extra sessions were held for those who needed and wanted extra help.

Many of these students would go back to communities where the English language is never spoken. Our goal was to help them learn some principles that would be useful in their ministry. Working with many, many students was an incredible privilege as well as responsibility. We write our memoirs telling of events and perceived accomplishments in our lives. Many of these students went out to adventures and achievements that would make our stories pale by comparison. Lola did not go along on my extra activity trips away from UBS. This permitted her to attend to her important work regularly. She had been trained in library technology. Her specific skills had to do with book repair. Many of the valuable books in a library are old books. Often professors put books on reserve as assigned reading for the course they are teaching. More than one student uses these books during the semester or the quarter. The next time that course is taught the same thing happens again. In this way books highly valued by the professors receive heavy wear. Often these books are checked out and taken to the students' rooms where they encounter some rough usage to regular wear and tear. Keeping all of the books in good repair and ready for use is an important aspect of library work.

The library at UBS had a large percentage of old books. Lola was faced with a constant flow of books to the repair desk. In addition to the actual hands on repair work, she taught students the art of book repair. In time her duties, in addition to her own repair work, included teaching, supervising and inspecting work done by others. Through the years she worked closely with others in the library and had contact with the students. This led to some lasting friendships.

UNION BIBLICAL SEMINARY MOVES TO PUNE

Union Biblical Seminary (UBS) began as a Free Methodist Bible School, but in 1953 officially became a union. Dr. Frank Kline and other mission leaders saw that individual missions could not afford to finance and provide personnel to operate a first-class theological school. These leaders decided to bring a number of different missions together to form a union. Several organizations working together could finance and provide staff for a seminary with capability to graduate Bachelor of Divinity level students.

The Free Methodist Mission in India offered a twenty-acre compound in Yavatmal as the place for locating the campus. Dr. Kline became the first principal. Different missions seconded professors to make up the faculty. All cooperating missions were asked to contribute to the budget. In time, more than 20 different missions joined in this union.

Students from all parts of India as well as from Japan, Maylasia, countries in Africa, and other lands of the world attended the seminary. The student body grew to more than 100 students. The school became known far and wide as Yavatmal Seminary. Having such a school in our India Free Methodist Headquarters was quite a feather in our cap. We provided faculty and made a sizeable grant to the annual budget. Add to this the fact that our denominational leadership was being trained here. Obviously, Free Methodists felt that a lions' share of the seminary's ownership belonged to them.

The Free Methodist Church in India turned over all of the land and buildings of the campus to the Union. Quite soon after the title was clearly in their name, the Board of Governor of UBS voted to sell the Yavatmal campus and move to Pune.

In fairness, it must be said that there were certain good reasons for wanting to move the seminary to a larger city. However good those reasons may have seemed to the other members of the seminary board, the idea of losing the school from Free Methodist headquarters was painful to say the least.

The final decision was made after a very great amount of discussion and negotiation. It is beyond by powers of description to make the magnitude of this matter real to someone who was not involved. The pros and cons were discussed in the Board of Governors' meetings. The matter was taken up by many different missionary boards in America. Dr. Kirkpatrick traveled to India to present the Free Methodist cause. Dr. Saphir Athyal traveled to Indianapolis to argue his position. It is no exaggeration to state that the weight of it all was so great as to affect that it affected Dr. Kirkpatrick's health. In the end, the move was carried out basically without Free Methodist approval.

In our letter of April 1983 we wrote, "Much of Gordon's time has been spent teaching at the Seminary. Lola gave much of her time to the library work, as well. The seminary's move will affect both of our lives deeply. Gordon is Mission Superintendent, Chairman of the Hospital Board, involved in many conference committees, and director of tribal evangelism – making it impossible for us to go to Pune."

YAVATMAL COLLEGE OF LEADERSHIP TRAINING

A growing number of people became concerned about the Yavatmal campus being vacated when the seminary moved to Pune. One of these men was Mr. P. Joshua, chairman of the Friends Missionary Prayer Band. He sat on the seminary Board of Governors and was one of the first to propose that the old campus be used for a missionary training school. Gordon heartily agreed with this idea. As he shared his thoughts with Dr. Narendra John, it was found that he too favored this idea.

Many outstanding graduates considered the old campus a sacred place. While earning their degree, they spent from three to five years there. Interacting with other students and with godly professors was a precious memory. What is more, they had been blessed in chapel services or in private prayer vigils, and had significant spiritual experiences while on that campus. Some of these former students, now become faculty, were willing to give leadership for founding a new school.

I had the privilege of sitting in on the early brainstorming sessions for founding the new school. The agreement with Union Biblical Seminary left five acres of the old campus to the Free Methodist Church. Our early thinking was to somehow manage with those acres and the buildings on them. Dr. Frank Kline urged us to trust for the total campus. On his advice, we began to dream on that level.

The seminary was asking us to pay a million dollars to buy back the campus. Nothing short of a miracle could make that possible. But God is in the business of doing miracles. We decided to proceed on the basis that He would do just that. Dr. Kirkpatrick, General Missionary Secretary, raised $200,000 for the initial payment. That was a magnificent start. A second big help was the fact that the seminary asked for payment in rupees. A certain exchange rate was effective at the time when the agreement was signed. In a year or two, the exchange rate changed so drastically that the payments we were required to make were greatly reduced.

The Seminary took everything they could. Everything that was loose was loaded onto trucks and hauled to Pune. That included chairs, desks, tables, and the like. Built-in cupboards were torn from the walls. Ceiling fans, as well as light fixtures, were removed from the ceilings. Fortunately, windows and doors were left intact. They considered that the property belonged to them and acted accordingly.

Names for the new school were considered. Yavatmal College of Missionary Training was the preferred name. The India Government frowned on the word "missionary." For that reason, the name Yavatmal College of Leadership Training was decided upon. The new school is generally known by its initials YCLT.

YCLT opened for classes in June 1984. Students had to sit on mats on the floor. To begin with, things were rather bleak. In His providence, God brought Bob and Judy Nugent into the picture. They helped form the home board known as India Missionary Training Board – in short, IMTB. Under their energetic leadership, funds were raised to pay off the indebtedness, to buy furniture, install fans, pay faculty, and basically to operate the new school.

From a small student body of 14 in 1984, the school has had marvelous growth. Below is information describing the ministry of YCLT at present. I quote from a recent letter written by the principal, Dr. Andrew Swamidoss.

"YCLT is located on a campus in central India previously occupied by Union Biblical Seminary, which is now relocated near Bombay. The campus, located on 20 acres, includes a chapel, staff quarters, dormitories, guest housing, library, office and classroom space. YCLT has over 80 students on campus, representing 22 denominations and twelve states in India. In addition, more than 70 students are taking courses in our new extension program. This program is designed to train and equip men and women who are already working as missionaries, but are unable to come to YCLT for residential studies owing to financial conditions or their presence being indispensable in the field. YCLT's classes are taught in both Hindi and English.The campus also houses two other entities closely related to the college:

1. An English-medium High School with over 1,800 students and 35 teachers

2. The Minerva Stewart Home which houses (provides room, board, education, health care and loving nurture to) 79 children whose parents are missionaries serving in remote or dangerous areas, representing 22 missionary organizations and 12 states of India.

PROGRAMS OF YCLT:

— A three-year Bachelor of Missiology degree

— A two-year diploma in missions

— A one-year certificate in missions

— A six-month certificate in missions"

OTHER EDUCATIONAL INSTITUTIONS

Up to then, mission-sponsored education was seen primarily as a means of helping children and adults read the Bible. For a number of reasons, Umri School was still providing education only through the seventh grade. To transfer from Umri School at that level, and enroll in a public school, was difficult. For that reason, people took their children out of our Christian school and put them in a Hindu school after the sixth grade. The results of this were not good, morally, spiritually or academically for our young people.

Umri Hospital needed doctors. The Free Methodist Church in India needed leaders. Our schools were not providing the academic foundation that would make it possible for our young people to go for higher education and prepare to fill these roles. As a member of the Umri School Board, I began to encourage members of the Board to seek government approval for upgrading the school. Over a period of years, we were able to bring the school up to the tenth grade. The equivalent to high school graduation. With this certificate, students can enroll in college.

The result of this change has been a large increase in the student body. The latest information I have is that more than 750 students are now attending Umri School. Hopefully, some of them have gone on to college and a few have returned to serve in their community and in their church.

In a similar way, I had some input regarding the English-medium school in Yavatmal. U.B.S. leadership recommended that the school be closed. In Board meetings and private discussion, I strongly recommended that we keep it open. I urged that we not only maintain the school, but also work at upgrading it from the lower grades to provide training through high school.

Hindus and Moslems prefer that the school have Christian management and faculty. Hindus would not send their children to a Moslem school, and Moslems would not send their children to a Hindu school. Both communities are happy to send their children to a Christian school. The well-to-do citizens of Yavatmal send their children to this school. They pay tuition sufficient to fund its operation costs. Since the school did not require mission support, it seemed obvious that we should not just keep the school open but also promote its improvement and advancement.

The result has been that Yavatmal English-medium School has become a prestigious institution, recognized as maintaining the highest academic levels of any school in the area. How effective it is for evangelism is not so clear. That it is an excellent public relations tool for YCLT and the Christian community cannot be doubted.

Some of my fondest memories of India relate to these two schools. In 1983, just before leaving India, I was invited to Umri School for a farewell. All of the boarding school students, as well as the day scholars, were there. What an attractive group they were with their sharp uniforms, bright eyes and well-oiled black hair glistening in the sun. More than 300 of them gathered in a meeting to express their love and thanks. Following the meeting, they lined up on either side of the road and waved goodbye to me as I slowly drove away.

In a similar fashion, as Lola and I prepared to make our final departure from Yavatmal, the boys and girls from the English Language school formed lines on both sides of the driveway to say goodbye. What wonderful send-offs these were!

Through the years, I had many students in my classes. Undoubtedly every teacher reflects on his or her influence. Even while I was teaching, I went on trips into the hills to minister to the tribes. I was asked to report on developments before the entire student body. My enthusiasm for actually reaching out and being directly involved in ministry was something the entire student body observed. Perhaps the Lord used that to encourage some who were considering missions or were half-hearted in their vision for ministry.

Since the two schools have been upgraded, thousands of boys and girls have attended and graduated. What small or large part has this played in the Lord's work? Certainly all of this is meaningless unless it was led of the Lord in the first place, and empowered by the Holy Spirit to bear fruit for His glory. Someday, in heaven, we shall join with countless others to see how our little part fits together into His divine plan.

A SNAPSHOT OF THE YEAR 1983

In the spring of 1983, we wrote as follows:

"Dear Friends:

What a time this past year has been. You will need to exercise your sense of humor, along with your heart of concern, as you read our blow-by-blow account of some of the highlights of the year.

In March 1982, Gordon was elected Chairman of the Board of Directors of Maharashtra Bible College. The same evening that he was notified of his election, rumors began to come to him of trouble between the principal and the registrar. Later, in the full meeting of the Board, both the principal and registrar were dismissed and the school closed for one year.

Later in the year, after applications for visas for David and Sherrill Yardy had been pending for several months, the sad news came that their visas were rejected.

About this time, we became aware that some of the workers at Umri Hospital had formed a union. It required several special Board meetings and considerable negotiation to get them to dissolve their union.

Not long after this, the full Board of Union Biblical Seminary met to consider whether or not to leave the English

B.Th. program in Yavatmal. The Free Methodist Mission strongly hoped that they would. For that reason, it was a great disappointment when the U.B.S. Board voted to move the entire program to Pune. A further shock came when Free Methodists met with U.B.S. representatives to negotiate a portion of the old campus with buildings for a continuing training program in Yavatmal. Except for five acres guaranteed in the deed, we were quoted high rates for any additional land and buildings on the land we chose. Since all of the land and many of the buildings in question were originally ours, this came as quite a jolt.

Finally, Dr. Pratap and Dr. Jennifer left Umri Hospital in December. We have been carrying on with one temporary doctor after another since then. Please believe us that your prayers, letters and cards have been a great help to sustain us through all of this, and we praise the Lord for the supply of His sustaining grace in answer to your prayers.

Man's disappointments are often God's appointments. We need to be alert to what God is saying to us in these events. He may be directing us to new thoughts about the ministries He has in mind for India.

On the brighter side:

Maharashtra Bible College will open again this June. David and Sherrill Yardy's visas are being applied for a second time. A young doctor has come to Umri and is applying to serve one year. He talks of serving five years. Plans are progressing for a continuing training program on a portion of the old U.B.S. campus.

Some present concerns:

Another doctor is needed to form a medical team at Umri Hospital. Wisdom is needed for directing Rev. Sidam in church planting among the Kolambs, and for Rev. Naik as he continues translation and literacy work in the Kolami language.

A report on family matters in 1983:

Gordon and Mary, with their three children, live on Bainbridge Island, Washington. He is in business and Mary is teaching in the public school. Their eldest daughter is blossoming into young womanhood as she approaches 14 years of age. They are giving thought to visiting us in India.

Larry and Kimi, with their children, live in San Diego, California. Larry's company was forced to shut down temporarily. He experienced a bit of unemployment, along with thousands of other Americans, at that time. Fortunately, he found a temporary job and recently his company called him back to work.

Wesley and Jean, with their two children, are back in Brazil where Wes is principal and Jean is English teacher in a school for missionary children. They are praying that the Lord will enable them to visit us in India this year.

Verle and Lois, with their two children, are in Dayton, Ohio, where Verle is completing his third year of service in the Psychiatric Ward of the hospital on Wright Patterson Air-Force Base. He faces setting up his own practice after July."

EPILOGUE

We formally retired from the work in India in 1983. The major part of our story concludes at that time. From that time to this, twenty years have gone by. Many things have happened in those twenty years. A brief synopsis follows.

YEAR OF DEPUTATION

We owned a two story, three bedroom house in the town Camden, Michigan, and we enjoyed living there whenever we could during that year.

Securing Visas for David and Sherrill Yardy and Family

After a year of extensive travel, I was asked by Dr. Kirkpartick to return to India briefly. In September 1984, I went to India with the main assignment to obtain a visa for David and Sherrill Yardy and their family. The final answer was, "No." I was back in Camden by mid-October.

ADAPTING TO LIFE IN AMERICA

We had from mid-October to the end of the year to find employment. Our lovely home in Camden was too expensive for us to maintain without an adequate income. We left mission work because of Lola's health. I was not yet of retirement age. We had neither mission income nor Social Security to help us at this time.

Nothing opened for us in Southern Michigan. Verle and Lois were living in Anchorage, Alaska at that time. He was associated with the Samaritan Counseling Center in Anchorage. He and Lois knew of our need and wished us to join them in Alaska. Verle felt that I could have an important ministry as a pastoral counselor.

FIFTEEN MONTHS IN ALASKA

We spent one year and three months in Anchorage. I learned many things that proved helpful later in life. The most valuable outcome was having a year near Verle, Lois and children. We had the special privilege of being present when their adopted son William was put in their arms.

LIFE IN SEATTLE

Things were not working out well for us in Anchorage. Life was very expensive, and we were dependent upon a heavy subsidy from Verle. The prospect of completing counselor training and being able to start my own practice was getting more and more remote. We decided to abandon that program and return to the lower 48 states.

Several avenues had to be considered. One was the possibility of a pastorate in Southern California. A second possibility was returning to Southern Michigan. The third possibility was in the Pacific Northwest Conference. The latter was the one that opened.

Rainier Avenue Church hired me to be visitation pastor, primarily for seniors. Rev. and Mrs. Eugene Stewart were planning to go to Africa for four years and offered to rent us their house for that period. This was the open door we decided to enter.

Wes and Jean were in Brazil. Verle and Lois were in Anchorage. None of our children were in Southern Michigan. On top of that, Lola's brother and sister, with their families, had moved to Texas. Reasons for returning to Michigan were greatly reduced. In addition, Gordon's brother Warren and his wife Elaine, as well as his sister Margaret and her husband Vern lived there. These were added attractions for the Seattle choice.

During those four years, we saw each of G.E.'s children– Stephanie, Ethan and Kendra –graduate from high school. These and other occasions to get together have meant much to us. Being on the West Coast made it easier for Larry and Kimi to come and visit us. We had opportunities to visit them in San Diego a few times as well.

Margaret and Vern often invited us to join with them, as well as with Warren and Elaine, for an evening of fellowship. We had numerous times when we played Skipbo or dominoes together.

THE MOVE TO WARM BEACH

The Stewarts were planning to return and take over their home in 1990. Providentially it worked out for us to move to Warm Beach Senior Community in June of that year.

A HUD subsidized apartment helped us financially, but we still needed more income. A job as bus driver for Victoria Village met that need.

CHAPLAIN OF WARM BEACH SENIOR COMMUNITY

In the course of events I was chosen as Chaplain at Warm Beach Senior Community. Lola and I enjoyed seven years in that office and consider those years as some of the finest years of our many years of ministy.

FAMILY GET-TOGETHERS

Since June of 1990, we have enjoyed a number of exciting family events. We went to visit Gordon and Mary and their family on Bainbridge Island many times. They, in turn, visited us at Warm Beach.

We were privileged to attend college events and gradu-ations for Stephanie, Ethan and Kendra. Also there were the weddings for Kendra and Eric, Ethan and Helen, as well as Ernie and Carina. Our health and the distance back east prevented us from attending the weddings of Sarah and Mike, Cheri and Michael, Matt and Karla, and Robert and Kathy. Videos and photographs helped somewhat to make up for the fact that we could not attend.

Through the years, Wes and Jean have come to visit us when they were on furlough. On those occasions our other sons and some of their family members also came to visit. These family reunions have been the highlights of our lives. We look forward to them and cherish the memories.

GOLDEN WEDDING ANNIVERSARY

Lola and I were to celebrate our Golden Wedding Anniversary in 1994. Gordon and Mary offered to finance a cruise or whatever we wanted to do for our celebration. We chose to reserve a "bed and breakfast" in the city of Hillsdale, Michigan, and plan the celebration to take place there. Many members of the original wedding party were able to be present. Two of Gordon's brothers were there, as well as many of our family and friends.

A BRIEF SUMMARY OF OUR FAMILY AFFAIRS IN 2010

On April 22, 2009 my beloved wife, Lola went to be with her Lord. She was suffering from much pain and feeling more and more handicapped. It was her fervent wish and prayer that the Lord would take her home. He graciously answered her prayers. Her departure leaves a huge vacant spot in my life, but I am thankful for the comfort and strength the Lord gives and for the support of Christian friends at Warm Beach Senior Community

G.E.(Gordon) and Mary live on Queen Anne Hill in Seattle, Washington. Mary continues to teach, although she now teaches younger teachers. Gordon is still in business as CEO of a software company. His company does bill collecting on behalf of doctors and clinics.

Gordon and Mary have three children, all of whom graduated from the University of Washington. Their brief story follows:

Their eldest daughter, Stephanie is still keenly involved in animal rights and works with the animal rights organization called PETA.

Their son Ethan is married to Helen. They live in Seattle and are now the proud parents of three sons. Several years ago, Ethan and a partner formed a software company that was very successful. Eventually he and his partner sold their business and now Ethan helps his father manage the company mentioned above.

The youngest daughter, Kendra married Eric Gil. They are blessed with a son and two daughters. Kendra and Eric have both earned their MD degrees and have recently signed contracts with a clinic in the Seattle area.

Larry and Kimi live in San Diego. Some time ago Larry retired from his work as a mechanic with U.S. Air. He has since contracted with H & R Block to help people with their tax returns.

Their son Ernie completed a degree in law. Ernie married Carina and they are the happy parents of a boy and girl. Ernie and Carina live in the San Diego area where Ernie works with a law firm and Carina is involved in banking.

Ernie's sister Emily has taken extensive training to help her cope with her blindness and has a meaningful ministry helping other unsighted students learn to read and write Braille efficiently.

Wesley and Jean are nearing the end of their missionary career in Brazil. At present they are located at Viannopolis, about a two-hour drive from Brasilia, the capitol. Wes teaches science and math and Jean is librarian and also teaches English. Wycliffe and New Tribes Missions have joined their schools together at this location.

Their eldest daughter, Sarah married Mike Gibula in 1995 before graduating from Taylor University in education and music. They have three children - two boys and a girl. Mike is employed by Verizon and has recently been transferred to Southern Indiana.

Their son Matthew graduated from Taylor University with a degree in engineering and physics. Matthew married Karla Dallaire in 2002 and they have three delightful little girls. Matt has retained employment as program engineer in the auto industry in spite of the economic crisis.

Verle and Lois live in Southwestern Michigan. Verle continues his practice as a psychiatrist. They make their home on a small farm. Verle hopes to continue the work he loves, God willing, for several years to come.

Their eldest daughter Cheri married Michael Fields. They are the happy parents of four children — three boys and a girl. They are currently living in a mobile home located on Verle & Lois's farm. Michael has recently taken an appointment as associate pastor of a church in the area. The senior pastor is seeking to groom someone to take over the work when he retires. With the Lord's blessing that will work out for Michael.

Cheri's brother Robert graduated from his course in engineering and is married to Cathy. Robert works as an engineer for an oil company and Cathy continues with research that will lead to a Ph.d.

The three younger children, William, Debra and Mary are studying and preparing for their life ahead.

SUMMARY

Lola and I cherish the joy of having a large family. We are rich in the truest meaning of that word. Our four sons are all married. They have given us twelve grandchildren. We have lived long enough to see most of our grandchildren married and having families of their own. To date, we have eight great-grandchildren and the ninth is expected in October.

As we write, we have 30 members in our family. They include a jet engine mechanic, teachers, doctors, a lawyer and successful businessmen. All have given us reason to be proud and give thanks to the Lord.

CHURCH GROWTH UP TO 1995

At the conclusion of "The Bombay Story," we mentioned that the Lord had greatly blessed the work there. At present, thirty congregations are reported with 2,000 members. An Annual Conference has been established and the work is going well.

God's blessing upon the work in Bombay has led to further expansion of Free Methodist ministry in India. The Lord provided leadership as the work in Bombay grew. This led mission leadership to believe that the same could happen wherever the Lord leads our church to minister.

On February 2, 2003, after 10 years of ministry, the churches in the city of Bangalore were declared a Provisional Annual Conference. Six congregations there have over 950 members. A congregation in the city of Guntur has been included in this provisional conference.

Rev. G. John, a graduate of Union Biblical Seminary, was led of the Lord to give his life to tribal ministry. He formed an organization that he named Agape Fellowship. At the close of a lifetime of ministry, he decided to bring Agape Fellowship under the Free Methodist umbrella. Included in his organization are more than 250 tribal congregations with an adult membership of 17,000 and with 6,000 junior members.

The latest Light and Life Magazine reports that 732 tribal churches from Immanuel Fellowship requested acceptance as part of the "India Free Methodist Church." This group has been accepted and is named "Immanual Conference." Included in this amalgamation are 60,000 parishioners. The result of this second, major merger is that the India Free Methodist Church now has more than 1,000 congregations with over 80,000 members. Needless to say, along with all of these new accessions has come a gigantic responsibility.

Yavatmal College of Leadership Training

College Students Missionary Children English Language School
1988 = 30+ Students 1988 = 30+ Students 1988 = 600+ Students
1995 = 90 Students 1995 = 75 Students 1995 = 1800 Students

Hundreds of students have been trained for ministry as rural pastors or as missionaries. Some of our most effective pastors at the present time are among these graduates. The results of the ministry of all of our graduates will only be told in eternity.

Umri:

Umri Christian Hospital

As has been true from the beginning, Umri Christian Hospital has its highs and lows. At times it has had an outstanding medical team. When that happened, the patient flow was large, the wards were full, and finances good. At times, excellent doctors were not available. During those times, the medical ministry waned. In spite of that fact, through the years hundreds of thousand of patients have found help. At the same time, the Gospel has been shared with all who come and go. Praise God we were able to keep it open during our watch, and this ministry still goes on.

A recent development has been a nursing school with 180 students.

OTHER INSTITUTIONS AT UMRI:

English Language School (320 Students)

Marathi Language School (700+ Students)

BOARDING SCOOLS ARE MAINTAINED IN:

Balharsha, Bangalore, Bombay, Guntur, and Umri.

Several hundred children are supported by Child Sponsorship.

UPDATED STATISTICAL REPORT TO 2010

THE TOTAL CHURCH MEMBERSHIP in India Free Methodist churches is now 128,671

OTHER EDUCATIONAL INSTITUTIONS –

UMRI: English Language School has 380 Students

Marathi Language School has 700+ Students

BOARDING SCHOOLS

Several hundred children are supported by Child Sponsorship in Balharsha, Bangalore, Bombay, Guntur, and Umri.

We have two hostels in Tamilnadu and one in beginning stages located in Latur. There are close to 1000 children in the Child Sponsorship program. We have built our own buildings at four locations at a cost of about $500,000.00.

Agape and Immanuel Conferences have several hostels and about twice the number sponsored children through their systems. Adding these brings the total to near 3,000 children in Free Methodist sponsorship programs.

Breinigsville, PA USA
13 July 2010
241673BV00001B/1/P